The Federal Manager's Guide to EEO

HECSA EEO

by

Robert J. Gilson

FPMI Communications, Inc.
707 Fiber Street
Huntsville, Alabama 35801

(205) 539-1850 • Fax: (205) 539-0911

ISBN 0-936295-29-5

Table of Contents

Chapter Two

Making The Selection Process Work

Chapter Three

Developing Employees

Chapter Four

Creating A Positive Work Environment

Chapter Five

Dealing With Discrimination Complaints

Chapter Six

Additional Information

Introduction

Introduction

This is the second edition of *The Federal Manager's Guide to EEO*. The primary changes between the first and second editions are to include new requirements concerning processing of EEO complaints as required by regulations issued by the Equal Employment Opportunity Commission. We have also added a new section in Chapter Five on alternative dispute resolution and how this process may affect the handling of EEO complaints in your agency.

As its title suggests, this book has been written to help managers and supervisors succeed in dealing with their Equal Employment Opportunity (EEO) responsibilities.

Many agencies also use the book for their EEO counselors and EEO professionals to provide an overview of the program from the perspective of the manager or supervisor and to give these EEO representatives ideas that may be useful in an agency in ensuring success of the agency's equal opportunity program.

The purpose of this book is to help you succeed as a manager by using the EEO program more effectively.

To make the EEO program work for you, it is necessary to learn what it is meant to do, how it is designed to work and, most importantly, how to recognize and responsibly deal with your EEO responsibilities.

The book provides an overview of the purposes, structure, and requirements of the Federal EEO program. It identifies situations in which supervisors and managers have clear responsibilities—and opportunities—under the EEO program and it outlines how to effectively meet EEO responsibilities.

Purpose

The purpose of this book is straightforward: To help you succeed as a manager by using the EEO program more effectively. Equal employment opportunity is an important goal of the Federal Government, and a variety of laws and policies impact the decisions of every Federal manager. And, because achieving EEO objectives is routinely included in agencies' performance rating systems for managers and supervisors, your career success or failure may be directly linked to how well you make the EEO program work.

Making EEO work in your organization is a realistic, achievable matter if you are able to recognize the opportunities that exist and take full advantage of the program to build a strong, effective workforce. But a successful EEO program will not just happen as the result of good intentions. To make this program work for you, you must learn what it is meant to do, how it is designed to work and, most importantly, how to recognize and responsibly deal with your EEO responsibilities. And that is where this book comes in.

Structure Of This Book

The Federal Manager's Guide To EEO has been organized to give you a full overview of the EEO program, while breaking out specific areas of responsibility for ease of review. Accordingly, in Chapter One you will learn the key features and requirements of the Federal EEO program, definitions of important terms, and an overview of your role in the program.

In Chapter One, you will learn the most common situations that bring your EEO responsibilities into play. In Chapter Two you will examine the requirements and opportunities that arise in making selection decisions. Chapter Three examines your role and the EEO implications of developing and training employees. Chapter Four looks into the specific requirements necessary to build a positive work environment free of sexual harassment or other discriminatory overtones. And in Chapter Five you will see how to respond effectively to EEO complaints and problems that might arise. The final chapter provides a useful summary of EEO terms and information you will need as a reference guide.

How To Use This Book

This book is not intended to make you a subject matter expert in the Federal equal opportunity program. Your agency already employs people who are experts in this area and they are available to help you deal with questions and problems that are bound to arise. This book should not be used to replace them or their advice and assistance.

The Federal Manager's Guide To EEO provides you with a basic, practical understanding of what the EEO program is, how it is intended to work, and what you must do to make it a success in your organization. Therefore, this book should be read—and reviewed from time to time—to help you to recognize situations in which you have EEO responsibilities, and to alert you to situations in which you should seek the assistance of your agency's experts.

Chapter One

The Federal Manager and EEO

Introduction

The key to the success of the Equal Employment Opportunity program in your organization is the operating supervisor and manager. The reason for this is easy to understand. Managers and supervisors make virtually all of the decisions that directly impact on the success—or failure—of any EEO program. You fill vacant positions and make selections for promotions; you approve training and detail employees to other positions; and you set the tone for dealings among employees in your portion of the organization. Higher levels can issue policy statements, but only operating managers and supervisors can make an EEO effort succeed. But in order to make it succeed, you must clearly understand what you should—and should not—be doing.

Objectives Of The Federal EEO Program

The objectives of the EEO program are straightforward. The first is to provide a full and fair opportunity for all employees, regardless of race, age, religion, sex, color, national origin, or handicap to contribute to the extent of their abilities in pursuing a career in the Federal service. The second is to provide for the non-discriminatory treatment of all employees in the course of carrying out their duties in the Federal workplace.

These two objectives require that employees not be unfairly limited in obtaining employment or in career advancement consistent with their performance and abilities, and that they be treated in a fair and non-discriminatory manner while performing their duties. This chapter will provide you with an overview of how these goals are met. In order to do so, it is first necessary to define some of the key terms used in the program.

What Is Discrimination?

Discrimination, in a general sense, means making a decision based on some distinguishing factor. For example, choosing only persons with operating experience as machinists to fill in for an absent machinist supervisor involves making a decision based on a discrimination factor: experience in a particular field.

Unlawful discrimination involves making decisions or treating people differently based on improper reasons—such as race, age, sex, color or national origin. These factors are not proper for making decisions because they have specifically been outlawed by a variety of Federal laws and regulations. Preventing *unlawful* discrimination is the primary purpose of the Federal EEO program. You are entitled—and even required—to use lawful discrimination (that is, judgment) in making many routine supervisory decisions.

For example, you may reward employees in your organization that are the best workers; that is, those that write the best reports, resolve the most problems, or somehow stand out because of their superior performance of their duties. This is a type of discrimination *but it is not unlawful discrimination.* It is a legitimate exercise of your managerial authority to reward your best employees.

Unlawful discrimination involves making decisions or treating people differently based on improper reasons—such as race, age, sex, color or national origin.

However, if you were to reward employees based on reasons or factors that have been prohibited by law and regulation, that is *unlawful discrimination.* For example, if you give awards only to employees who are under 45 because you want to encourage younger employees to do a good job, you are using an employee's *age* as a reason for making a personnel decision. This is unlawful discrimination because an employee's age is not a legitimate factor for deciding who gets, or does not get, an award.

What Is Prohibited Discrimination?

The next step to understanding the goals of the Federal EEO program is knowing specifically what constitutes prohibited discrimination, how it is identified, and the options available to managers to cope with discrimination in the workplace. The remainder of this chapter covers the prohibited factors constituting unlawful discrimination under Federal law and the factors you, as a Federal manager or supervisor, should avoid when making personnel decisions.

Race And Color

Race is a matter of scientific definition. Anthropology classifies human beings by body type, facial features, bone structure, etc. Generally this determines whether a person is classified as belonging to one race or another. Examples of racial groups would include Caucasian (white), Negro (black), and Oriental.

Color refers to a person's actual skin shade, and may constitute a separate discrimination factor regardless of a person's race. For example, persons on the Indian subcontinent may have dark skin although they are classified by anthropologists as Caucasian or white. Similarly, many American blacks are actually fair-skinned. Discrimination based on skin color, regardless of race, is also prohibited by law and regulation.

Sex And Sexual Harassment

Both men and women may claim discrimination because of their sex. If a person is not considered for a position or a promotion specifically because of gender, that decision would be unlawful discrimination based on sex.

A second kind of sex discrimination is generally called *sexual harassment*. Although definitions vary under different agency regulations, in general sexual harassment consists of unwanted and inappropriate sexual advances, consideration of sexual favors in making personnel decisions, or creation of a hostile environment in the workplace through remarks and jokes of a sexual nature.

A person may claim that superiors or co-workers have made sexual advances a condition of keeping or advancing in a job, or in some other way have created a job environment hostile to a particular sex or to an individual. An agency which permits prohibited harassment to occur without taking steps to stop it may be found to have tolerated sexual harassment in the workplace.

Both men and women may claim discrimination because of their sex. If a person is not considered for a position or a promotion specifically because of gender, that decision would be unlawful discrimination based on sex.

Sexual harassment may consist of:

- •• Direct demands for sexual favors.

- •• Unwelcome sexual activity directed to employees.

- •• Personnel decisions based at least in part on whether employees have cooperated with sexual initiatives.

- •• Creation of an offensive work environment in which employees are intimidated or believe they may be disadvantaged by the sexually-oriented behavior of supervisors or other employees.

As a Federal supervisor, you are responsible for knowing what is going on in your organization and for taking steps to ensure that sexual harassment does not occur. Failing to take appropriate action to prevent sexual harassment may result in your agency being found responsible for tolerating an atmosphere that condones or tolerates sexual harassment.

Sexual preference—that is, heterosexual or homosexual—is not a specifically prohibited basis of discrimination. Discrimination on the basis of sexual preference could serve as the basis for a grievance or appeal as it is a non-merit factor under civil service law.

Religion

This refers to a person's religious beliefs—or lack of them—or a person's membership in a religious group. Using this factor as the basis for personnel decisions or the treatment of a person in the workplace is also prohibited. Employees may raise religion as the basis of a complaint either because they are treated differently as a result of their religious beliefs, or because the agency is failing to make a reasonable accommodation of needs required by the person's religion.

For more information, see *The Federal Manager's Guide to Preventing Sexual Harassment,* © 1992 by FPMI Communications, Inc., Huntsville, AL, and *Sexual Harassment and the Federal Employee,* © 1992 by FPMI Communications, Inc.

For example, an employee could claim that a supervisor is treating an employee differently in making assignments or performance ratings because of the supervisor's own religious beliefs. Similarly, an employee may complain as the result of a supervisor refusing to allow an employee to decline an overtime assignment on a Sunday based on a religious prohibition of work on that day.

National Origin

As the name suggests, national origin as a basis for discrimination involves making decisions or treating a person differently based on a person's country of origin. These complaints are often based on treatment perceived to be influenced by a person's last name, accent or cultural heritage. The key, again, is perception of different treatment and suspicion of different or unfair treatment growing from statements, jokes or other indications of bias.

Age

Only people over 40 may allege age discrimination using EEO complaint procedures. It is unlawful discrimination either to create a benefit or a disadvantage for a person because of age. For example, telling a person who is 45 years old that you are looking for someone more mature is discrimination. Similarly, telling a person who is 65 that you are seeking a more youthful image in your workforce is also discrimination.

An employee who is over 40 may allege discrimination against anyone who is younger. For example, a person who is 55 may allege she was the subject of discrimination when an agency selected an employee who was 53 for a promotion. *In other words, age discrimination does not always involve one person who is over 40 and another who is under 40.*

Unlawful Discrimination Factors

❑ **Race** ❑ **Color**

❑ **Sex** ❑ **Age**

❑ **Religion** ❑ **National Orgin**

❑ **Physical or Mental Handicap**

Sexual Orientation

Discrimination based on sexual orientation is not specifically prohibited by statute or the regulations of the Equal Employment Opportunity Commission.

The Equal Employment Opportunity Commission has ruled that sexual harassment or sex based discrimination is illegal regardless of the gender of the parties involved.

A number of agency heads have published policy statements prohibiting discrimination on the basis of sexual orientation in their agencies.

Presumably, an employee who wishes to complain of such discrimination would be able to file a grievance over the matter.

Civil Service Law (5 USC 2301 and 2302) establishs merit system principles that encourage recruitment based solely on relative ability and retention. This is based on the adequacy of an employee's performance while prohibiting discrimination based on any conduct that does not adversely affect a worker's own performance or that of another.

Physical And Mental Handicapping Conditions

The Rehabilitation Act carefully defines a handicapped individual as "any person who:

- ➤ has a physical or mental impairment which substantially limits one or more of such person's major life activities,

- ➤ has a record of such an impairment, or

- ➤ is regarded as having such an impairment."

The same law requires "reasonable accommodation" of these persons. Making a decision based on a person's disability—such as a promotion decision, for example—without considering the person's ability to perform the duties, may constitute handicap discrimination. The requirement to "reasonably accommodate" a person's disability is discussed in more detail in a later chapter.

Kinds of Discrimination

Now that you know the prohibited bases on which an employee may complain of discrimination, you should also know that there are two kinds of discrimination recognized by the courts, *disparate treatment* and *disparate impact*. But what do these two terms really mean?

Disparate Treatment

An allegation of *disparate treatment* is the one you are most likely to confront as a Federal supervisor. In making an allegation of disparate treatment, a person claims that he or she was treated differently from other employees of a different race, color, sex, age, or who were not disabled. An example of this might arise in a situation in which an employee who is disciplined claims that he or she received a more severe penalty for the misconduct than have other employees of different race, age or sex.

Disparate Impact

The second type of discrimination recognized by the courts is an allegation of *disparate impact*. An allegation of disparate impact most often focuses on a system (such as promotion, training, or entrance examination) that appears to treat everyone alike, but has the effect of harming a particular group. This kind of claim may be made either by an individual or a group. If made on behalf of a group, it is called a *class action* complaint.

For example, if a test is given to all employees in your organization to determine the knowledge and skill level in order to qualify them for promotion to certain occupations, your first reaction may be to assume there is no basis for discrimination because *all* employees are required to take the test. But if the test produces results in which only 50 percent of Hispanic employees score 70 or higher while 80% of non-Hispanics score 70 or higher, there may be a basis for finding the test discriminatory in its impact. As you might imagine, you are unlikely to become directly involved in such issues.

Discrimination Defenses

To defend against an allegation of *disparate treatment*, the employer must show it had a legitimate, non-discriminatory reason to take an action. In the example of the disciplinary action used above, the manager may make the defense that the employee who was disciplined received a more severe penalty because the misconduct resulted in greater harm to the agency or because the employee had a worse record of disciplinary offenses than other employees.

Defending against *disparate impact* claims is much more difficult and often involves statistical studies and complicated validations of the systems the employer uses. In the example above, the employer would probably have to prove that the test directly measures ability needed to do the job; that it accurately predicts future performance success; and that a test which produces a lesser impact on Hispanics would not be as effective in identifying successful candidates for the occupations.

Under-Representation

In seeking a workplace that provides a full and fair employment opportunity, the Federal government uses a variety of tools. One of the most important is a simple determination of the numbers of employees in various protected EEO categories in comparison to the numbers of such persons available in the workforce. For example, a survey might be made to determine how many females and minorities are employed in a particular occupation, such as computer programmer, in comparison to the number of such persons available to do such work. If the number of people available greatly exceeds the number employed in the occupation within the government or a particular agency, it may be determined that women and minorities are *under-represented* in that particular occupation. Similarly, it may be determined that women or minorities are generally under-represented in an organization. If so, various steps are called for to bring the workforce into balance. One such step is called *affirmative employment*.

What Is Affirmative Employment?

Boiled down to its essentials, affirmative employment (sometimes called affirmative action) is a conscious, deliberate effort to make certain that qualified minority and female employees are given a full and fair opportunity to be represented in—and progress in—the agency's workforce. To do so, managers and supervisors of an agency must take a variety of positive steps to ensure that they are encouraged to apply for positions, to give them full and fair consideration for positions on the basis of their qualifications and abilities, and to make a conscious effort to select them from the list of eligible qualified candidates to achieve better workforce balance.

Affirmative employment is a conscious, deliberate effort to make certain that qualified minority and female employees are given a full and fair opportunity to be represented in—and progress in—the agency's workforce.

In deciding whether affirmative employment is necessary, the most important consideration is whether a group is fully represented in the workforce. If it is determined that under-representation exists, the agency may adopt specific goals and timetables in an effort to close the employment gap. In making decisions to set goals and targets related to employment decisions, agencies look at the percentages of minority, female and disabled employees at various grade levels and job types. Affirmative employment plans are not required to address age or religion, although a court finding a pattern of discrimination may order specific actions taken to correct a problem.

Goals Vs. Quotas

A number of tools are used in the affirmative employment program. Among them is establishing employment goals to overcome under-representation. The use of such goals has been controversial, and has raised the question of whether the action itself is discrimination against other groups that are not benefiting from the program.

At the heart of such problems is a basic misunderstanding of the difference between the terms *goal* and *quota*. In considering this problem, you need to understand the difference. A *goal* is an objective toward which an agency works. It is *not* a mandatory number that must be met regardless of employee qualifications. A quota is a mandatory number that must be filled, usually by a specific date.

In general, although agencies routinely establish specific goals for the employment of women and minorities, they generally avoid establishing quotas. Consequently, contrary to a common misunderstanding, a supervisor is not required to hire specific types of employees regardless of qualifications.

Special Emphasis Programs

Another tool used in accomplishing affirmative employment is that of the special emphasis program. These programs are directed at improving employment opportunities for particular groups, and they are encouraged and required by regulation. Specific efforts of a special emphasis program may include targeting resources and identifying specific individuals to benefit from the resources available. The Federal Women's Program, Hispanic Employment Program and the Handicap Placement Program, are all identified in regulation and addressed in affirmative employment plans.

Upward Mobility

Often the cornerstone of an internal EEO program, *upward mobility* involves the use of an alternative approach to traditional ways of filling jobs through promotion. Under most upward mobility programs, intermediate positions—usually known as "bridge positions"—are established. To gain the experience and training necessary to qualify for a higher level job, a training plan is developed to allow employees who do not normally qualify for a target job. For example, a personnel assistant position may be created as a "bridge position" to enable a clerical employee to develop the qualifications necessary to progress into a personnel specialist position.

Special Recruiting Authorities

A person with a disability or a cultural disadvantage may also be the beneficiary of a number of special placement arrangements. These programs allow an agency to hire a person who would not normally qualify for Federal employment. For example, an agency may use a "special handicap appointment" to offer a person an opportunity to begin work for the government. After a period of time, a person hired under this program may receive the normal benefits of civil service employment. Another such program is the student/summer aide program for the economically disadvantaged. This program allows outstanding students to work for the Federal Government while still in school and to have an opportunity to gain work experience—and possibly a full-time job with an agency after graduation.

Your agency's personnel specialists can provide further information about such programs and how you can use these programs to have a successful Equal Employment Opportunity program in your organization.

Obtaining Additional Resources

Affirmative employment successes are often tied to the willingness of a particular manager to take a chance and try to implement a program in the organization. You may find that you can obtain additional resources in money or positions if you are willing to hire a disabled worker or restructure one of your positions for placement through upward mobility.

Who Me, A Model Manager?

This book is designed to help managers such as yourself identify opportunities and implement a practical, successful equal employment opportunity program at your worksite. EEO is a highly visible program, and one that is widely perceived as being difficult to implement. In reality, however, all it requires to be successful is the combination of two factors: Basic knowledge of the tools available, and a desire to succeed. The purpose of this book is to provide help with the first. But it is up to you to put these and your own ideas into practice.

Getting Help

For advice on affirmative employment, upward mobility and other EEO and personnel matters, contact your Equal Employment Opportunity or Personnel Office. In some agencies, these programs are in the same organization.

EEO specialists plan for affirmative employment and manage special emphasis programs. Personnel specialists are routinely involved in filling vacancies, structuring positions, providing training and performance advice as well as defending management actions.

Get a briefing from these specialists on what your agency's specific EEO and Affirmative Employment Programs involve, and what services are available to you to successfully manage your organization.

KEY POINTS

•• Discrimination on the basis of race, color, religion, national origin, age sex or handicapping condition is prohibited by *law*.

•• Discrimination based on job related factors such as performance, training or experience is proper and the basis of sound management decision making.

•• There are tools available to managers to make Equal Employment Opportunity work for you while avoiding unlawful discrimination.

•• The key to success in EEO is your *desire* to make the program work for you and your employees.

Chapter Two

Making the Selection Process Work

Introduction

Using the selection process effectively is one of your most important functions as a successful manager or supervisor. After all, it is through your selection of employees that you determine the strength of your most important resource: the people who work for you. It is also a key situation in meeting your EEO objectives in that it provides an opportunity to employ affirmative action in balancing your workforce. Becoming known as a manager who makes solid, objective selection decisions based on qualifications, while remaining sensitive to EEO objectives will enhance your credibility with employees and agency management, and will help you develop a reputation as a fair and unbiased manager.

Making sound selection decisions based on the qualifications of applicants while taking into account EEO goals and objectives requires both substantial knowledge and serious effort on your part. This chapter will familiarize you with the selection process and point out where EEO opportunities—and problems—can occur.

Getting Organized

If there is a vacancy under your supervision, you should be thoroughly involved in the process of filling the position. To do so you must be aware of the options available to the selecting official, regardless of whether you or another manager will make the final decision. You may have more alternatives than you realize.

Options

A vacancy may be filled in a number of ways. For example, it may be filled by promoting one of your current employees; by reassignment of an employee at the same grade level; by transfering an employee from another part of the organization; by selecting a candidate from a register maintained by the Office of Personnel Management; by reinstating a former Federal employee; or by selecting of a candidate through competitive procedures under the agency's merit promotion plan.

In addition, you have the option either of selecting an employee who is already fully qualified and able to perform the full range of duties in a position or choosing a new employee with only basic qualifications, but who will require substantial training. For example, such an employee might be a new hire from outside the government; or a disabled worker who may require making changes to an existing job to accommodate a person's disability; or an upward mobility candidate selected through your agency's upward mobility program. Although OPM regulations require competition for most new hires and promotions, in other cases you will find that you have flexibility in deciding how to fill a position. Your agency's personnel specialists can help you to identify specific programs available for filling a position in any particular situation.

Filling a Job

In building an effective EEO program for your organization, filling vacancies with qualified people is critical to your efforts. As you probably know, you can't simply offer a job to a person you have decided you want to hire. Law and regulations require that you take an organized and objective approach to filling job vacancies. Therefore, before you fill a job, you need to take several key steps.

Initial Steps

First, plan ahead for vacancies. Although it is not always possible to predict which employees will leave in the next year, it helps to think about how you would replace them if any of them should leave you with a vacant position. In planning ahead, carefully review the requirements of positions under your supervision so you can develop a clear idea of the qualifications necessary to satisfactorily perform each job. Then, in planning ahead, recognize that it will often be in the organization's best interests to fill jobs at a lower level and develop employees to the full performance level over a period of years. This approach will reduce turnover and ensure development of the skills and knowledge your organization requires.

Second, once a vacancy occurs, talk with an agency personnel or staffing specialist, describing the vacancy you have and the qualifications you need to fill the position. Ask the specialist to advise you of your options in filling the position; the recruiting sources available for the position; the lead time necessary to fill the job using various options; whether it would be practical to re-structure the job to permit filling at a lower grade level; and whether there are any applications for reassignment or transfer on hand.

Third, think about the EEO implications of filling the job. Ask yourself if your workforce is balanced with men and women, minorities and non-minorities, Hispanics, orientals or other groups appropriate for your geographic region. Review or ask about the agency's affirmative employment plan or commitments for your organization, and determine whether it may be necessary to take steps to enlarge the number of candidates to attract qualified minority or female employees.

Fourth, if you have a number of similar jobs at the same grade level, consider using the agency's upward mobility program or one of its other special hiring programs to fill at least one position per year.

Talk with the personnel specialist for your organization before filling your job vacancy. In this way, you will learn about all of your options and you will be able to fully consider the EEO implications of filling the job.

Fifth, once you have decided on an appropriate method to seek candidates for the vacancy, work closely with your personnel specialist to ensure that you meet all requirements in objectively and fairly assessing their qualifications, and in properly selecting on the basis of qualifications.

Key Steps to Filling a Job

1. Plan ahead for vacancies

2. Talk to your staffing specialist

3. Think about EEO implications of filling the job

4. Consider special hiring programs

5. Talk to your personnel specialist to ensure you follow all steps to properly select an employee

If You Recruit From Outside. . .

As discussed above, one of your options is to recruit applicants from outside your organization, from outside the agency, or even from outside the Federal Government. It will always be in your interest to attract minority, female and disabled applicants for jobs you need to fill. Depending on the location of your organization, the nature of the work, the local job market, wage and salary levels and other such factors, you will have varying choices. Know what your choices are and how practical it may be to use a particular recruiting method or source. For example, how long will it take to have a new employee report to work using a particular method to fill a job? How much will it cost to recruit from different sources outside the Federal Government or outside your agency? Considering these factors, what will be the overall benefit of using one method instead of another?

Deciding whether to seek a fully trained worker instead of a new employee that will have to be trained, or whether to hire an employee from outside rather than promoting from within is not easy. Such factors as the impact on the morale of current employees, the cost of finding minorities, women, or disabled applicants and whether the person you hire would require training must be weighed before you make a final decision.

Avoiding Problems Up Front

Identifying the qualifications and requirements associated with a job, and making them clear to potential applicants will help to avoid many of the problems supervisors encounter in filling vacancies. Be sure to have your personnel office include in any vacancy announcement special requirements of your job, such as overtime requirements, shift work, travel requirements, physical requirements such as heavy lifting, or other unusual working conditions. Applicants will appreciate having this information in deciding whether to apply for the position. And you will benefit by having fewer misunderstandings over job requirements with the person ultimately selected for the position.

Promotion From Within

When you decide to fill from inside the organization through promotion, attention must be paid to equal opportunity concerns, since promotions are by far the most common actions challenged in discrimination complaints. For example, if you decide to hire from outside your organization, and qualified minority or female employees are already working for

"Be sure to have your personnel office include in any vacancy announcement special requirements of your job, such as overtime requirements, shift work, travel requirements, physical requirements such as heavy lifting, or other unusual working conditions."

you or other supervisors in your unit, a complainant may question why you decided to hire someone who is not as familiar with the organization and the job requirements. If you have a good reason for hiring from outside, and have considered and rejected the option of promoting from within for good cause, you are free to fill the job as you wish. Under these circumstances it is a good idea to document your reasons at the time the decision is made.

If You Rate and Rank...

If a job is to be filled by using the agency's merit promotion plan, the position vacancy is usually advertised for a specified period of time, during which interested candidates may file applications. After the end of the posting period, a group of agency employees and/or supervisors will be organized to read, rate and rank the applications. Nor surprisingly, these groups are called *rating panels*.

At one time or another most managers will be called upon to rate and rank candidates for a job by sitting on a rating panel. Although some agencies may use a staffing specialist from the personnel office both to determine applicants' basic eligibility for a job and to rate and rank them, it is more common for a panel to rate the candidates.

The Rating Process

This process generally begins with an initial screening of candidates' applications by a personnel specialist to determine whether an applicant is at least basically qualified for the vacant position. Eligible candidates' applications are then rated by the panel, which uses a *crediting plan*. A crediting plan is a document—prepared in advance—that assigns point scores for knowledge or experience critical for performing a job. Raters carefully review each eligible applicant's background and assign points for knowledge, skill and ability based on the experience, education, training, performance appraisals, awards, and other job-related factors reflected in their applications.

A rating panel is a group of agency employees that is usually asked to rate and rank candidates for a job.

Each panel member's score for a candidate is then compared to those of the other raters and averaged to develop a single overall score for each applicant. The job candidates are then ranked in order according to their scores. Finally, applicants' names are placed on a *certificate* that is forwarded to the selecting official for consideration.

To limit the number of applicants under consideration, the certificate may also be divided into *qualified* and *best qualified* categories. Some agencies add an additional step of a *recommending or selection panel* to interview candidates and forward their recommended choice to the selecting official.

EEO Implications of Rating and Ranking Applicants

Personnel staffing specialists usually decide the eligibility of applicants. Questions or complaints about basic eligibility determinations are normally directed to the personnel office.

Because managers usually rate and rank the eligible applicants, complaints that a person was not given the correct number of points based on their experience and qualifications are usually aimed at the rating panel or members on it. For example, a job applicant may claim that the crediting plan itself, certain factors or elements in the plan, or the points awarded to an individual, are incorrect or unfair or discriminate against a particular individual or group.

Therefore, it is important to document how and why you and the panel reached each decision, and to be prepared to explain what you did and why you did it. If records are kept centrally, it is probably a good idea to keep notes on key decisions for your own records as well.

If You Select. . .

After all eligible candidates for a position have been rated and ranked, a certificate is prepared and sent to the *selecting official*—that is, the person with the authority to choose which person will be selected for the job. If you are the selecting official, you will be faced with the problem of determining which of the persons to pick for your position. If you have several well qualified candidates, this can be a difficult task. And it is important to recognize key EEO considerations while making your decision in order to head off potential problems later.

Distinguishing Factors

Once candidates have been fairly and objectively rated, it is up to the selecting official to determine which candidate best matches the specified job requirement. Usually this involves a factor-by-factor comparison of the candidates to determine the overall best qualified. Sometimes it may involve weighing one factor more heavily than others in determining the best qualified candidate.

In making your selection, it is both proper—and necessary—to rely on particular distinguishing factors to decide which candidate is best suited for the

job. For example, in filling an engineering technician position that will involve extensive work on
lighting systems, you may lean toward an applicant
with more direct experience working on such projects. Or you may give preference to a candidate
with more background on a particular kind of print-
ing press, if that is the kind of equipment that will
be used in the job. Such distinctions are legal, proper, and completely up to you to decide upon.

The only distinguishing factors you **cannot** use are
those that are prohibited by law—race, age, sex,
handicapping condition, color, religion or national
origin. And the key to avoiding falling into the trap
of using such considerations in choosing among
candidates is to examine carefully the reasons you
are leaning for or against particular applicants. For
example, if you want an employee with solid math
skills for a job, that's fine. But if you are inclined
not to select a female applicant simply because you
feel women as a group are less capable in using
mathematics, you are relying on a prohibited factor—sex—in making your decision.

Avoid Using Prohibited Factors

**1. Recognize the factors you are using and
ensure they are job-related.**

2. Evaluate candidates using objective factors

The best way to avoid letting prohibited factors influence your decision is by 1) recognizing the factors you are relying upon and making sure they are directly job related; and 2) evaluating candidates' qualifications in light of objective distinguishing factors—**not** pre-conceived notions of the ability of an entire group. To follow the example one step further, a person's mathematical ability as a distinguishing factor is fine if it is an important feature of the job. But women applicants—as well as men— should each be considered based on objective evidence of their individual math skill, not ruled out on the assumption that they are automatically less qualified than men.

Being Aware Of Agency Goals And Objectives

A related question you may be wondering about is whether it is okay to consider race, age, sex or other factors as a **positive** element in considering a candidate. So long as such factors are not used to select an unqualified or less qualified person, the answer is "yes."

To illustrate, if you have two roughly equally qualified candidates for a position, and either would fully meet the particular selection factors you feel are important for the job, it is legal and appropriate for you to take into consideration both your agency's affirmative action goals and the candidates' individual status in making your decision. Indeed, doing so is at the heart of achieving a balanced workforce.

Deciding Based On Objective Criteria

If one particular candidate is clearly superior, regardless of whether he or she is in a protected group, that person should be selected. On the other hand, if two or more candidates are roughly equally qualified, you are free to choose either. In such circumstances it is also permissible to consider your affirmative action goals in making the selection decision from among equally qualified candidates.

To defend your decision in the EEO complaint process, you will have to show a legitimate, non-discriminatory reason for picking the person selected for the job. This sometimes creates problems for a supervisor or manager. For example, if you select a candidate based on the performance of the winning candidate, but the complainant has an *outstanding* performance rating, you are likely to be found guilty of having engaged in discrimination even though you stated a non-discriminatory reason for your action. The best way to do this is by using objective selection criteria.

Note that you are not required by the EEO program, the affirmative action plan, or the agency's merit promotion plan to disregard qualifications or to pick unqualified or less qualified persons. You are only required to make a full, fair and objective evaluation of candidates and to select from among them without bias.

Do Yourself A Favor: Keep Notes

Finally, once you have reached a decision and selected from among the qualified candidates for a position, it is a good idea to write a brief memorandum detailing how and why you reached your decision. Include the factors you used; why the selectee was the best overall choice based on these factors; and how these factors are the key to successful job performance. Get in the habit of drawing up such notes whenever you are involved in making a selection, and keep them in your own records. They can be extremely helpful in refreshing your memory if you are faced with explaining your decision a year or more later!

Talking to employees who were not selected to let them know why another person was selected and how they can improve chances for selection for future positions is also a good idea. If a person knows what occurred and why, it can also reduce the chances of a complaint being filed about the selection process.

Keep notes about your thought process when you made your selection for a job. Also, let any candidates who were not selected know how they can improve their chances for selection for future openings that may occur.

Interviewing

To Interview Or Not

The decision to interview may already have been made for you. Some agencies require an interview in all promotions, or in all selections at or above certain levels. Agency rules may also require that if you interview one candidate, you must then interview all. Ask a personnel staffing specialist about your agency's rules on selection and make yourself a list of *do's* and *do not's* based on the specific rules used in your agency.

If you do have the option of deciding whether to interview applicants, however, there are a number of factors to consider. Included among them are the following:

••• If all candidates are employees from your organization, you may not need to interview if you already have enough information—based on their applications, performance appraisals and your personal observations of past performance—to make a selection.

••• If one candidate is clearly superior in qualifications to the other applicants after rating under the crediting plan, you may not need to conduct interviews.

••• When there are well-qualified outside candidates, or internal candidates who are unknown to you, interviews usually make sense.

•• When you are concerned that applicants may not feel they have received a full and fair opportunity to demonstrate their qualifications without an interview, it is often a good idea to interview.

•• When several well qualified candidates are referred to you and the differences among them are minor or not apparent, an interview may prove helpful in identifying the best applicant.

•• Morale of internal applicants should be a key factor in your decision to interview. Give current employees the chance to demonstrate their abilities.

Organizing The Interview

If you do decide to interview candidates, the interviews must be fair, objective and directly job related. To make certain interviews are conducted correctly, follow an organized approach to the interviews.

This checklist will help you to set up and conduct fair, effective interviews that will steer clear of potential EEO problems.

1. Prepare your questions in advance and write them down.

2. Review each question to make certain that it is tied to a specific, job-related selection factor.

3. Do not ask questions that are not job-related or that reflect an irrelevant value—such as a personal belief in the importance of mothers remaining home with small children. Needless to say, avoid any question that appears culturally or racially motivated, or that reflects a sex, age or handicap bias. Examples of the kinds of questions to avoid include the following:

➤ Are you able to communicate with whites?

➤ As a Hispanic, do you feel you will be able to fit in?

➤ Do you plan to have children?

➤ Is your career tied to your spouse's?

➤ Will your spouse object to your travelling with men, women, blacks, whites?

➤ How soon do you intend to retire?

➤ Do you think you can get to work on time considering your . . . . (disability)?

4. If an interviewing panel is used, assign specific questions to each panel member and do not allow panel members to make up questions as they go. Doing so can result in questions that are not truly job-related, and it can result in some candidates being subjected to different and tougher—or easier—interviews than others.

5. Ask the identical questions of each interviewee. While there will be differences between candidates, remember that the interview is a test. Make it a fair one.

With this in mind, think for a moment about what interview questions you might ask of applicants for a clerk-typist position. A list of sample questions that might be developed before beginning interviews is included below for your review.

SAMPLE INTERVIEW QUESTIONS

Position: Clerk-typist GS-4

Factor 1. Knowledge of filing structures

We use the _____ filing system. Have you worked with it before? When? For how long? What do you feel are its strengths and weaknesses? What other filing systems have you worked with? Please describe them. What technical information was involved? Have you received any formal training in filing systems? When? Where? How has that training helped you in your previous positions?

Factor 2. Knowledge of administrative functions

What experience do you have in handling and routing mail? In arranging for government travel? Preparing orders? Completing vouchers? Have you been responsible for ordering and stocking supplies? What experience have you had in recording time and attendance? What work schedules did you work with? How many employees were involved? Have you worked with a word processor or computer-based word processing system? Which ones? How long did you work with each system?

Factor 3. Ability to work with minimal supervision

How was work organized in your previous office? To whom did you report? How frequently did your immediate supervisor provide direct instructions and feedback? On what matters were you required to obtain permission before carrying out a decision? What matters were completely within your discretion?

As you can see there is a lot to cover in a job-related, goal-oriented interview. Notice that every question in the example above is designed to provide the interviewer with valuable, job-related information. Equally important, no questions were asked that would indicate bias or the use of selection factors not truly related to the job. In such interviews, applicants may feel assured that the decision will be based on valid, job-related elements, and objective qualifications, not on personal prejudices.

KEY POINTS

•• Selecting employees for open positions is one of the most important duties of supervisors and managers, and one of the key opportunities for building an effective EEO program.

•• Think and plan ahead about how you will fill vacancies that may occur in your work unit.

•• Your agency's personnel specialists can help inform you of a wide variety of ways in which you can fill vacancies when they occur. You should evaluate them in light of practical considerations and their usefulness in helping you to meet affirmative action and EEO goals.

•• Crediting plans and selection criteria are used to make hiring decisions. It is essential that the crediting plan and selection criteria used in filling positions be directly related to the requirements of a position, and that they be applied in the same way to all applicants.

•• Selecting officials should carefully consider whether to interview qualified candidates before making a selection. If interviews are conducted, it is important to key the interview questions to the specific job-related criteria. Avoid non-job related questions, or questions that could be viewed as indicating a bias for or against any group.

•• Document your thoughts, reasoning and actions carefully and completely at the time decisions are made during the selection process.

Chapter Three

Developing Employees

Introduction

One of the criticisms levelled at the equal employment opportunity program is that it is a "giveaway program" designed to benefit protected groups at the expense of others. But that is neither its intent nor the way you should use it.

What the law envisions and what you should work toward as a Federal supervisor, is a system that is based on job performance. A system that does not show preference to—or bias against—any person because of factors such as race, age or sex. Under this system, you should strive to allow everyone an equal opportunity to succeed, and you should make your personnel-related decisions based on a person's achievements on the job. This chapter explains how to set and communicate realistic job expectations, how to help employees to meet these expectations, and how to take appropriate action based on employees' performance.

Your Expectations

Rarely does anyone walk into a job and immediately perform at a full performance level. Most of us must go through a process that includes learning about the organization, its staff, and its rules and goals while we are learning how to perform the full range of duties at hand. Most employees learn their jobs through a lengthy process of trying, succeeding—sometimes failing—and trying again. Unfortunately, this approach to the developing employees is a haphazard affair in which individuals either make it—or fail—on their own. The cost to the agency of employee failure is high when the time, productivity loss, recruiting and replacement costs are factored in.

To succeed as a supervisor, it is essential that you recognize employees will have varying levels of ability, skill and experience. Not all of them will be capable of "hitting the ground running" upon entering your work unit. Therefore, it is an important part of your job as a supervisor to help develop employees to the limit of their abilities—both for their benefit and that of the organization. How you do that, of course, is the $64,000 question.

In this chapter you will learn how to develop employees' skills effectively, and with a systematic approach that will help enhance your EEO program while helping you to get the most from your subordinates.

Identifying Expectations

The key to building and maintaining a competent work unit is the setting and meeting of clear expectations for employees. These expectations fall into two general areas: on-the-job performance, and conduct. Each is explained in more detail on the following pages.

"The key to building and maintaining a competent work unit is the setting and meeting of clear expectations for employees."

Getting Off to a Good Start: Establishing A Performance Plan*

Effective employee development starts with your efforts to bring an employee up to full performance level and the limit of their potential within the job he or she currently occupies. And in order to do that you first need a clear idea of exactly what the job is, what skills, knowledge and abilities are required, and what constitutes good performance. After all, if you do not know what it is you want employees to be able to do, how can you develop or rate them?

Establishing Performance Requirements

Knowing what a particular job involves and precisely what you expect the person in the job to accomplish is the bedrock starting point in the process of developing employees. You can develop this information by following a few simple steps.* They include the following:

1. First, list the essential duties of a particular job. You can get a handle on this by reviewing the position description for the job, discussing the job with experienced employees or other supervisors, and thinking about the important things you want ac-

---

* For more information on developing and writing effective performance standards, see *Performance Standards Made Simple!: A Practical Guide for Federal Managers and Supervisors,* (Third Edition) FPMI Communications, Inc. (1991).

complished by any person who holds the position. If performance plans have been previously developed for the position, the job elements you identified in the performance plans will give you a head start on this process.

2. Under each main job duty, list the specific tasks that have to be accomplished in order to perform in an acceptable way. For example, if the specific duty is preparing travel orders, the individual tasks might include obtaining the proper authorization numbers, determining the correct per diem amounts for disbursement of travel advances, and arranging lowest cost travel arrangements.

<u>Keys to Good Performance</u>

1. List the essential duties

2. List the tasks required

3. Determine how well each task must be performed

4. Identify the most important tasks

---

3. Determine how well each duty and task must be performed in order to be satisfactory and better. This usually involves specifying the quantity, quality and timeliness requirements for accomplishment of a duty or task.

4. Identify which specific tasks are the most important duties. These are usually referred to as the "critical elements" of the job, and are the duties that the employee absolutely must perform satisfactorily in order to remain in the position.

Having done all this, you now should have a clear idea of what it is that you expect *any* employee occupying a particular job—regardless of age, race or sex—to accomplish. The next step, of course, is communicating your expectations to employees.

Communicating Performance Expectations

You may remember a movie from several years ago in which a "manager" who is having a difficult time with an "employee" explains the problem by saying that "What we have here is a failure to communicate." Actually the failure to communicate clearly is at the bottom of many on-the-job problems, and at the heart of many EEO complaints. In establishing performance expectations and developing employees to meet them, it is essential to communicate clearly and often.

The first step, of course, is to sit down with employees who work under your supervision and outline what you expect them to do, and how well, quickly or often you expect them to do it. If they see any problems with doing so, or understand the job to involve other duties you have not mentioned, both of you will have an excellent opportunity to get a clear mutual understanding established.

On the other hand, if you determine, based on your conversation with the employee, that he needs additional training or development in order to meet your performance expectations, you can work out a plan to overcome any potential performance deficiencies. Usually such development plans involve specific additional training or developmental experiences. This is covered in more detail later in this chapter.

Outlining for employees what you expect them to do and how you expect them to do it is an on-going job of a supervisor and it is one of the first steps in the performance process.

Finally, once you and the employee have reached a clear understanding of what he is expected to accomplish, it becomes your responsibility to monitor the employee's performance, to provide counseling and feedback, and to provide assistance necessary to bring performance to the desired level.

In reviewing and carrying out these steps, note that the key point is to establish clear, objective, well-understood job requirements that apply to *any* employee regardless of race, age, or sex. The development of performance standards and the fair, even-handed use of them in rating employees provides the cornerstone for a discrimination-free system of supervising, evaluating, rewarding and promoting employees.

> **"The development of...performance standards and the fair, even-handed use of them in rating employees provides the cornerstone for a discrimination-free system of supervising, evaluating, rewarding and promoting employees."**

Setting Conduct Expectations

The second area necessary to establish a clear understanding of your expectations with employees is that of *conduct*. Conduct refers to the specific standards of behavior that you require employees to meet in connection with their work. For example, requiring that employees be at their work stations at the official starting time, that they refrain from using profanity in dealing with agency clients, and that they personally call in to obtain approval for sick leave, are all work rules, or standards of conduct that you might apply. It is a good idea to make certain that all employees under your supervision understand the basic rules you apply in the workplace. You can make sure they do, of course, through a variety of methods, including one-on-one discussions, posting notices, or spreading the word through supervisory meetings.

The key to successful, non-discriminatory management of employees is, first, making all employees aware of the same rules, and second, applying the rules in an even-handed manner. Failing to accomplish one or both of these steps frequently results in suspicions of—and complaints about—discriminatory behavior.

For example, if you were to allow women employees to take long lunch hours without comment, but reprimanded men for the same activity, it may appear that you are biased in favor of the female employees. Similarly, if you discipline a black employee for using profanity but have tolerated such language from white employees, your treatment is likely to be viewed as discriminatory.

Keys to Successful Management

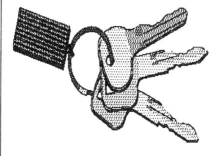

Make all employees aware of workplace rules

Apply the rules equally

Deciding which matters to cover with employees will depend, of course, on the needs of your particular organization. The following checklist provides a list of some things you may want to include:

1. Work hours, including starting and quitting times, lunch and break periods, and how strictly they are enforced.

2. Leave policies, including requirements for obtaining advance approval, call-in policy when sick, and the like.

3. Security of information, equipment and documents. In other words what should be locked up, and what should not be discussed at home or casually with persons outside the work unit.

4. Who is important to your organization, why they count, and how clients are to be handled; for example, telephone etiquette, or proper methods of addressing military officers.

5. What is acceptable in office manners and culture. Language, dress, office decorations, private use of the telephone and similar matters.

6. Important work procedures, such as how to obtain a car from the motor pool, how to format a particular report, or how to obtain access to security data.

You may even want to put together an information sheet with all the important facts on it. This will serve as a guide for you and will be of help for the new employee. How much did you remember of what you were told on your first day at work? Probably not much, because there is a lot to learn and a lot of new people to meet and remember. An information sheet will be used by virtually all of your new employees to try and remember what you told them and why it is important.

And remember, new workers are not the only ones who need to know the rules. Be sure to cover problem areas in staff meetings. Reminding employees of your expectations throughout the year is a good management practice to develop.

Dealing With Conduct Problems

Although making employees aware of your conduct requirements will head off the majority of potential problems, do not be surprised if some problems eventually crop up. When they do, it is important in dealing with them to be just as even-handed, methodical and professional as you are in setting performance standards. When you believe a problem is starting to develop:*

•• Promptly tell the person exactly what the problem is.

•• Tell the employee why it is a problem.

•• Tell the employee how you want it fixed. That is, what you want her to do in the future.

•• Listen carefully to what the employee says and be sympathetic, but be firm in demanding that your requirements be met.

•• Follow up your discussion with a written note to the person if you believe the problem may not end with a simple discussion.

•• Be prepared to take formal action if your discussion does not produce the desired results.

---

* See *The Federal Manager's Guide to Discipline*, Second Edition, FPMI Communications, Inc. (1991).

Building For The Future

Developing employees obviously involves more than just laying out performance and conduct expectations and then making certain they are met. It also requires you to think of ways of preparing subordinates to grow in responsibility and value to your agency. And after the thought, it requires effective action on your part. In short, it requires you to become a positive force in helping employees realize their full potential. But how do you do that? Actually, it's not as hard as it sounds, and there are plenty of resources available to help you.

Identifying Strong And Weak Points

If you are actively involved in directing and supervising employees, it should not take long to recognize their abilities, what they are good at, what they are interested in doing, and where they need improvement. As you develop and refine your assessment of each employee's strengths and weaknesses, interests and abilities, you should summarize them briefly and discuss them with each employee. In these discussions, you should determine the employee's career goals, interest in other positions or duties, and willingness to accept further responsibility or training. By the end of these discussions, you should have a clear picture of what will be required for the employee to progress, both in his or her present job and in future positions in the agency.

Setting Up Individual Development Plans

Once you have developed a clear idea of what skills or knowledge need strengthening to develop an employee's potential, map out a plan of action to attain of specific goals. In conjunction with the employee, and perhaps with the assistance of an employee development specialist from the personnel office, identify and schedule the specific training, developmental assignments and projects that will help meet the objectives you and the employee have developed. In doing so, you are also boosting the employee's motivation, helping to develop his or her potential, and increasing the value of your agency's most important asset—its employees.

For example, if an employee needs to produce better organized and written reports to progress in her current job and become eligible for other positions, you might schedule specific training in report writing skills and periodically review progress with the employee. Similarly, other weaknesses can be turned into strengths for her benefit and to the benefit of the agency.

Upward Mobility Options

In reviewing employees' interests and abilities for developing a comprehensive development plan, another tool you should consider using is the *Upward Mobility* program. Actually, Upward Mobility is not a single program. It is a variety of options available to a manager to recruit from among underrepresented groups when traditional sources do not provide adequate numbers of candidates.

In conjunction with the employee, and perhaps with the assistance of an employee development specialist from the personnel office, you can identify and schedule the specific training, developmental assignments and projects that will help meet the objectives you and the employee have developed.

In Upward Mobility, the key phrases to focus upon are *underutilized employees* and *dead end positions*. An *underutilized employee* is one who shows potential beyond his ability to perform within the current job's limits. A *dead end position* is one from which there is no career track or path to a higher level. When underutilized employees wind up in dead end positions, Upward Mobility provides a means for the agency and the employee to tap the unused potential.

Upward Mobility Creates Paths And Tracks

Moving employees from dead end jobs into higher level jobs requires planning and the use of what are usually called *paths* or *tracks*.

To illustrate how this process works, consider the example of a Supply Clerk (GS-4). Normally there is no way for an employee in this kind of position to progress to a Supply Specialist position, since the specialist positions usually require a college degree or experience at a level few clerks are able to attain. Most Supply Specialist positions are recruited at GS-5 with potential for promotion to the GS-11 level, while the Clerk position may be dead ended at the GS-4 level.

An Upward Mobility Program specialist may examine the situation to determine if a sufficient number of these positions exist in the agency's geographic area to warrant establishing a position that "bridges" the two jobs. An example of such a *bridge position* may be a Supply Technician job at the GS 5, 6, or 7 grade level. Although unable to qualify for the higher Supply Specialist positions, GS-4 Supply

Clerks could apply for the bridge Technician jobs at the GS-5 level, and be trained and developed to reach full performance at the GS-7 level.

After an employee has accumulated the necessary knowledge and experience through performance in the Supply Technician job, she may then have a chance to qualify for entrance into the Supply Specialist job leading on up to a GS-11. Thus upward mobility can be used to capitalize on employees' abilities and ambitions while meeting the agency's staffing needs.

As in all of the efforts that have been discussed, thorough planning is the key to a successful program. These are the steps to follow for implementing an upward mobility program in your organization:

1. Identify the position or positions in your organization that are dead ended.

2. Identify the employees who are underutilized.

3. Meet with EEO officials and Personnel Staffing specialists experienced with Upward Mobility programs. Use their advice and assistance to help you determine whether you can establish an effective Upward Mobility position in your organization.

4. Let these specialists know that you are willing to try an Upward Mobility effort and that you are interested in other Upward Mobility programs your agency may already have in place.

5. Work with the specialists to:

•• Restructure jobs as necessary

•• Establish training plans

•• Set performance goals at each stage of development

•• Prepare fall back plans if the candidate is unsuccessful

•• Create a support system for the participants that includes career counseling by professionals, assigning them to journey level workers who can help them perform and keep you informed on their progress.

Becoming A Mentor

A *mentor* to the ancient Greeks was a teacher and developer of the skills of youth. The relationship of a master tradesman and apprentice is built on a similar concept. But what does that have to do with you?

If you want to be successful at Equal Employment Opportunity in the Federal service, one of the best ways of doing it is by becoming a mentor to your subordinates and helping them to succeed. To do so you must go the extra mile in counseling, training and developing them. You must level with them. Let them know their shortcomings and their strengths. Be objective with them, and have a plan that they can understand and follow. Most of all, you must show them that you care both about them and their career goals. If you do, you will not only meet your EEO goals, you will also greatly increase your personal satisfaction in carrying out your responsibilities.

KEY POINTS

•• The key to developing employees is making performance and conduct expectations clear to all employees, and applying them consistently.

•• In dealing with performance and conduct problems it is important to act promptly and evenhandedly in requiring employees to live up to established performance standards and conduct rules.

•• Developing employees also involves an aggressive effort to identify employees' strengths, weaknesses, interests and potential in order to develop a sound, workable development plan.

•• Among the developmental tools that can be used are training, details, and rotational or developmental assignments.

•• An additional developmental tool available to help employees reach their full potential is the upward mobility program. Trained specialists are available to help supervisors and managers to develop upward mobility positions, identify candidates, and design a developmental program.

•• Using the full range of employee development tools will help you to meet your EEO goals and increase job satisfaction.

Chapter Four

Creating a
Positive Work
Environment

Introduction

Once the work force for the federal government was fairly predictable. Only men occupied certain jobs, and women occupied others. Similarly, black and hispanic workers tended to be clustered into specific positions, as were disabled employees. By looking at a position title, a person could make a fairly accurate guess about what categories of people would occupy the jobs.

Today, the only certainty is that the government is committed to a diverse working population that accurately reflects our society. In the federal government, traditional stereotypes are rapidly changing. And these changes make it necessary to come to grips with our own conflicting values and opinions. Long held opinions about sex roles, racial stereotypes, ethnic differences, and capabilities of people with disabilities must be evaluated in light of objective, first hand experience. And our opinions must be subjected to our own careful scrutiny as each of us—managers and employees alike—deal with the growing diversity surrounding us.

Handling Differences

This is not just a book for white male managers. It is for all of us, because equal employment opportunity is the responsibility of every supervisor, manager and employee. And all of us, regardless of our sex, race, culture or disability, are likely to have some pre-conceived notions. Some of these notions are appropriate and form the basis for our personal work ethic and our idea of what is required to do the job. For example, we may approach work with the idea that it is right to expect an employee to work productively regardless of whether a supervisor is watching over her shoulder. That idea may have formed in your home when you were a child, and it underlies your approach to work. It is also fully appropriate.

But all of us are also subject to ideas about entire groups of people who are different from us. It is easy to form or adopt ideas of what all members of a group are like, how they think and act, and what they can or can't do. Often, we are not even aware that we have categorized an entire group of people in this way. But when we do, we are forming *prejudices* or *biases*. In doing so we are literally pre-judging people and their ability based simply on the color of their skin, their accent, or their sex. That's bad enough, but when we *act* on such pre-formed ideas—rather than evaluating and reacting to the individual employee's performance and conduct—we are discriminating in an improper manner.

The Key Player

Whether employees feel they are getting a fair shake based on their actual abilities and performance depends to a great extent on the individual supervisor and manager. Your attitudes, the way you speak to and deal with individual employees, set the tone for your organization. If your apparent attitude and dealings with employees are fair, objective and even-handed, you will have a positive work environment. On the other hand, if employees come to believe—rightly or wrongly—that you treat them differently based on their race, color, creed, sex, age, disability or other improper considerations, you will preside over an unhappy workplace. And in such an environment you can expect your personnel decisions to be routinely challenged, based on employees' convictions that prejudice guides your actions.

Clearly then, the key to success is your need to recognize and root out both decisions and behavior that are based—or even appear to be based—on discriminatory prejudice rather than objective facts. Individual attitudes obviously are not easy to overcome, and few of us are perfect in this or any other way. *But the key point to remember is that the successful manager is careful never to let prejudice for or against any group to influence her work decisions—and never to allow her actions to suggest to employees that bias plays a part .*

In this chapter we will look at the concepts, ideas and values that can inhibit our ability to deal with employees objectively, and lay out some strategies for dealing with them effectively in building a positive work environment.

Solving Problems Based on Facts

The first step in dealing with values and biases that might interfere with our decision-making is to identify them. Get them out into the open so that you can deal with them. Often our reaction to others is driven by attitudes or values we may not even be aware of. Sometimes a negative reaction is rooted in the fact that an individual acts, dresses or speaks differently. In such cases we may have a negative reaction to an employee, but may not know why. To make certain your reaction is based on valid, job-related factors and not simply on the racial characteristics or cultural aspects of the employee's group, it is helpful to ask a number of questions:

1. What is producing the negative reaction? Is it specific behavior or actions of the employee, or is it the way the employee looks, speaks, dresses or handles herself?

If it is not based on behavior, there is a good chance that you may be reacting to the employee's cultural heritage and difference from you.

2. If the negative reaction is caused by specific behavior, does the behavior affect the employee's performance in any way, or is it in violation of workplace rules?

If not, the negative reaction may be rooted in cultural preferences and biases.

3. If the behavior is interfering with the employee's or others' performance of duties, the next step is...

A. List the specific things the person is doing—or not doing.

B. Identify which employees are affected by the actions.

C. Specify why the behavior is unacceptable.

D. Determine exactly how you want the person to conduct himself or herself.

4. At this point you have prepared an objective statement of the problem you are experiencing. The next step is to double check to see if the problem is genuinely based on valid, job-related factors or merely on personal biases. To do so ask yourself the following questions:

A. Would the same behavior be acceptable if a different person or a person from a different group did it? If so, the problem may be more one of group prejudice than actual behavior.

B. What makes the behavior negative? How does it impact on the employee's performance of duties? If there is no tie-in to actual performance of work, your reaction may be more personal than objective.

C. Is the problem cultural? That is, are you bothered by the employee's speech, jargon, accent or language? If so, is it traceable to the person's cultural background? Does the employee's speech pattern interfere with the performance of work? If not, your unease may be based on differences in culture, not ability or performance.

D. Is the problem based on the employee's mannerisms, etiquette, or style? If so, do they get in the way of the employee successfully carrying out job duties? If they do—such as offending agency customers—you have a legitimate problem. If not, it is probably a matter of personal preference and cultural difference.

E. Do you see the behavior as being inappropriate only for a member of the opposite sex? If so, you may be reacting to sexual stereotypes or your own cultural attitudes about the proper role and behavior of women—or men—rather than to valid, job-related issues.

F. If a disabled worker is the employee involved, does the employee's disability enter into the problem? Would the same behavior or performance by an unimpaired person be more acceptable? If so, personal unease with the employee's disability may be affecting your perceptions and decisions.

Evaluating Your Answers

As a manager, your task is to get the job done and to carry out your organization's policies effectively and efficiently. Most of the issues raised by the questions above relate to a *subjective* versus *objective* approach on your part. That is, to personal feelings as opposed to objective, job-related issues. If, in analyzing your approach to an employee, your answers indicate that you may be acting based on the way you personally feel about various groups rather than on objective, job-related facts, it is time to re-evaluate your stance. What follows are a few practical **do's** and *do not's* for every manager when it comes to EEO matters. First general areas are considered followed by specific suggestions for dealing with groups of people.

Generally

To create a positive work environment:

•• Let everybody know that you are opposed to discrimination, and act like it.

•• Treat all employees doing the same job alike. There are obviously differences between individual people, but the rules should be applied the same way for all.

•• Try to keep your personal opinions on non-work issues to yourself. Too often they may suggest to employees that your decisions are colored by personal convictions or biases, even if that is not the case.

•◆ Avoid assumptions about entire groups of people. Saying that you think that all blacks or women or Irish are this way or that is a guarantee of trouble. At the very least, it will make employees leery of working for you.

•◆ Do not tell or condone jokes directed at any ethnic, racial, sexual, religious or age group in the workplace. Managers' involvement in or tolerance of such matters has often been accepted by courts as evidence of discrimination or a discriminatory attitude.

•◆ Do not patronize employees of any particular group. Employees generally resent a supervisor stating how much he or she understands the problems "you people" have faced.

•◆ Avoid using emotional terms. Referring to the "girls" or "boys" in your organization, or using any prejudiced term such as "spic" or "wop" reflects an attitude that will be noticed and resented by employees. If you are the subject of an EEO complaint, any use of these terms will usually be brought out during the investigation of the complaint.

About Minorities (If You're Not...)

•◆ Being black, hispanic, or oriental is a fact, not a condition. Since there is no inherent difference between races, do not assume or emphasize perceived differences by attempting to use jargon or mannerisms you think belong to the group. What you see on television picturing various group stereotypes is just that—a stereotype.

About Whites (If You`re Not...)

•• Identical advice applies.

Men And Women

•• Never physically touch a subordinate or co-worker unless it is required by the job or you are specifically asked to do so by that person.

•• Sexual harassment is not confined to touching a person. Sexually suggestive gestures, jokes, remarks and other evidence of a sexual approach to employees have been the cause of numerous sexual harassment claims and supervisory discipline.

•• Never make a management decision based on the sex of a worker unless gender is a legitimate qualifying factor. Make sure it is a legitimate factor by checking first with personnel or EEO officials.

•• Deal promptly and decisively with any allegations of sexual misconduct in the office. Failing to do so makes you a party to the conduct. Again, for assistance, feel free to call on your personnel and EEO officials.

Workers With Disabilities

•• Do not assume that a disabled person is any less capable than any other employee. Although minor adjustments in the physical layout of the workplace may be necessary to accommodate a disabled employee, many supervisors have found that the abilities and productivity of such a person will often meet or exceed that of other employees.

•• Do not assume that a disabled person needs special assistance unless you are expert in the matter. If the person needs anything additional to get the job done he will ask for it. If so, simply get it, if possible, and get on with getting the job done.

•• If you have reason to believe employee performance is affected by alcohol or drug use, refer the worker to your agency's employee assistance program and seek assistance from your personnel staff on how to deal with the problem. Alcohol and drug abuse are "handicapping conditions" under the law and may require special consideration of the employee in dealing with the problem.

The Kind Of Place You Would Like To Work

If you do your best to make certain that your attitudes and—most importantly—your decisions are shaped by objective facts based on individual employees' performance and behavior, you will create a work environment free of actual or perceived discrimination. It will be a place where employees feel they are treated with respect, as individuals, and based on what they do—not on what group they were born into. In short, you will have created the kind of place where anyone—including yourself—would like to work.

If your attitudes and decisions are shaped by facts based on performance and behavior, you will create a work environment free of discrimination where people are treated with respect based on what they do—not on what group they were born into. You will have created the kind of place where everyone would like to work.

KEY POINTS

•• The individual manager or supervisor is the key to developing a work environment free of discrimination.

•• In creating a positive work environment, recognize that most people are subject to attitudes and expectations about entire groups of people. Such attitudes are called biases or prejudices.

•• Successful managers and supervisors strive to make decisions based on objective facts not the manager's personal biases.

•• The key to avoiding decisions based on personal biases is examination of personal attitudes, and careful review of the basis for your reactions to employees.

•• Although there are stereotypes about every possible group of employees, such generalizations are not reliable and cannot be the basis of effective decision-making. It is important to react to real, individual people, not to a television notion of what their group is like.

•• If you diligently seek to create a positive, discrimination-free work environment you will produce the kind of place where you and all other employees would like to work.

Chapter Five

Dealing With Discrimination Complaints

Introduction

No matter how well you perform in meeting EEO goals or in advancing anti-discrimination policies, the possibility exists that an employee or an outside job applicant may perceive an action or decision as being discriminatory. What then? Usually a discrimination complaint. Unfortunately for many managers, dealing with a discrimination complaint can be a confusing, difficult situation. In this chapter, you will learn how you can deal with these complaints in a professional, positive manner.

First Things First: Get Your Reaction Under Control

In dealing with any complaint, your goal should be to resolve the complaint in a way that is fair to the complainant, acceptable to you and perceived by the rest of your employees as an appropriate outcome.

The first and most important step in meeting that objective requires dealing with your own feelings toward the complaint and complainant. It should not surprise anyone that a person charged with discrimination may feel angry, or disappointed. This is particularly true when the decision you made (and which is now being challenged) was motivated in whole or in part by an intent to achieve an affirmative employment goal, or when the complaint comes from someone you know or have helped. Nevertheless, to deal with the issue successfully, you need to put those feelings behind you and deal with the issue on its merits.

Although a complaint may initially disappoint and even anger you, do not take it personally. Remember that while complaints are not inevitable, they may be viewed as another cost of doing business. That means getting the facts, listening carefully to understand why the person feels he or she was treated improperly, and then doing your best to work the matter out in the minimum time required.

Being careful to treat a complainant in a polite, businesslike and professional manner will not only help you resolve the complaint, it will also help avoid the filing of later complaints claiming reprisal against the employee because of the first complaint.

"Although a complaint may initially disappoint and even anger you, do not take it personally. Deal with it as business. And that means getting the facts, listening carefully to understand why the person feels he or she was treated improperly, and then doing your best to work the matter out in the minimum time required."

And, before getting too upset, it may help to keep in mind that unless your agency or the courts decide otherwise, the complaint is only a claim or an *allegation* that reflects the perception of a situation by an individual. Allegations, of course, are often incorrect, and must be supported by facts. They may also be refuted by facts. Therefore, your role in the process is largely one of finding the important facts and clearly communicating them to the complainant and those processing the case. Remember, the complaint is always filed against your agency and not against you personally. **While it may be alleged that you acted for the agency, you and your agency are always "innocent until proven guilty."**

Get Your Thoughts Together

In this chapter you will learn how complaints are handled and your role in the process. But before getting into that, there are several steps you should take when you become aware that one of your decisions—such as a promotion selection—may be challenged:

1. Review the decision in question and your actions leading up to it.

Jot down a brief outline, since you may not be asked about the matter for some time.

2. Gather any documents that relate to the matter, make copies and file them where you can find them later.

For example, if you relied in part on applicants' answers to specific interview questions, pull together any documentation of their answers.

3. Make a list of the people involved in the situation, their roles and knowledge of the action.

For example, if an employee has claimed that you disciplined him or her for discriminatory reasons, assemble a list of persons who may have been witnesses to the offense for which the person was disciplined.

4. Compose your thoughts on the challenged decision and, if not already documented, write down the reasons for your decision.

Unfortunately, discrimination complaints can take a long time to process, and your memory of important details may dim. Get your thought processes on paper now, while they are still fresh.

Understanding How the Process Works

Discrimination complaints go through various stages. The law provides for *administrative handling* before the *complainant* (the person who filed the complaint) is permitted to challenge an action in the courts. *Administrative handling* means the way your agency and the Equal Employment Opportunity Commission deal with an allegation of discrimination within the agency itself. Be sure to read the last section in this chapter on alternative dispute resolution (ADR) as this may affect how a case is handled in your agency.

The EEO Counselor

A person who believes he or she was adversely affected by discrimination must contact an EEO Counselor within 45 days of the incident on which the allegation is based to attempt to resolve the problem informally. *Most complaints are resolved at this stage in the process.*

The EEO counselor's job is to find out what happened and to try to iron out the problem. In essence, this requires gathering facts and getting back with the person who sought counselling. The counselor then shares the facts that have been developed with the employee. Upon learning all the facts involved, the person who sought counselling may drop the discrimination charge.

If the person who sought counselling still believes discrimination occurred after hearing the counselor's report, the counselor may contact the manager or supervisor involved, explain the problem, and try to work out an informal settlement. This is another point at which matters are often resolved.

Dealing With The Counselor

It is the job of an EEO Counselor to try to resolve potential complaints. *A counselor does not represent a complaining employee, nor serve as an investigator or prosecutor.* The EEO Counselor is trained to find out what is troubling the employee making the allegation, and to try to satisfy the employee in a way that is fair to all parties involved.

However, a person who seeks EEO counselling is entitled to have his or her identity remain unknown until a formal complaint has been filed. When the person wishes to remain unknown, the EEO Counselor obviously has a more difficult job. In part, the counsellor's job is made more difficult because other people, including the supervisor or manager, are often less willing to be helpful when the identity of the person who sought counselling is unknown. *In these cases, try to be as helpful as you can while recognizing the limitations placed on the counselor.*

Meeting With The Counselor

When an EEO counselor requests a meeting with you, prepare carefully. At the time the meeting is scheduled ask the counselor what will be discussed, and what information will be needed.

If you are the person against whom the complaint is filed (often known as the Responsible Management Official or other similar term), you are entitled to the following information, and you should ask for it if it is not provided to you:

1. What specific action or decision is alleged to be discriminatory?

2. What is the claimed basis or reason for the alleged discriminatory conduct (race, color, religion etc.)?

3. What facts support the allegation? What makes the person believe he or she was the subject of discrimination?

4. What action on your part would result in withdrawal of the allegation?

NOTE: At one time, a manager charged with discrimination was called the ADO or Alleged Discriminating Official. Agencies now refer to such managers as the Responsible Management Official (RMO) or other similar term.

A Note On Formality

EEO counseling is an informal process. You should not be asked to make sworn statements or affidavits at this point. If you are asked to do so, call the EEO Director or specialist in your part of the agency and explain the problem. Ask such officials if they consider it mandatory that you complete a formal statement. Ask to see a copy of your agency's EEO regulations, and ask where in the regulation it requires such statements. If no one is able to answer your questions on this point, consult with your agency's personnel and/ or legal office for their opinion. If all else fails you may want to seek outside (private) legal advice. (More about your rights later).

Where Does Your Boss Fit In?

Common sense dictates that you should keep your supervisor informed of what is happening at each stage in the process. Seek her counsel and assistance before making any commitments to settle the case. Use your boss and the management network to identify others who have had similar allegations to see how they have handled them. Also, find out what limitations, if any, your supervisor may want to place on a settlement offer.

The Next Step

If this informal process fails to resolve the problem within 30 days, the EEO Counselor is required to notify the complainant that he has 15 days in which to file a formal complaint of discrimination. The notice also advises the employee of where to file the complaint, and what information must be included in it. In short, the person who sought counselling is faced with the choice of dropping the matter or carrying it to a more formal stage. If the employee decides to go forward with the matter and files a formal complaint, the next step is full investigation of the claim if the agency accepts it as a complaint.

Dealing With An Investigator

The larger your agency, the more likely the investigation will be carried out by someone who conducts EEO investigations on a full time basis. An agency has 180 days from the filing of the complaint to investigate the complaint and issue a report. You should be thoroughly prepared to meet with the investigator and to make the strongest possible case for your position.

How should you prepare for an investigation? You are likely to fare better by taking a systematic approach such as this:

1. **Ask your EEO Officials for a copy of the complaint**.

As the RMO you are entitled to such information, and should not be shy about asking for it.

2. **Analyze the allegation**.

Carefully review the claimed facts for accuracy and completeness. Look for unsupported statements of fact, for inaccurate or incomplete facts, or conclusions that are simply not correct. People, including complainants, often have only a partial or incorrect understanding of the facts. Spotting them early can help you in working out a solution by providing a broader picture to the complainant later.

3. **Identify the specific decision or action that the complainant contends was improper**.

If the allegation simply contends that your overall attitude is the basis for the complaint, seek specific examples leading to that conclusion. You should not have to guess about what you have allegedly done.

4. **Put all relevant documents and notes in chronological order.**

Doing so now will later help you to present a clear, understandable picture of what has happened.

5. **Ask for assistance from your agency's EEO advocates**.

They are usually the attorneys or personnel specialists who will represent agency management if the matter goes to a hearing. These individuals have experience in preparing affidavits and other evidence, and will be able to help you prepare any statement you might give.

When it is time to give your statement to the complaint investigator, follow these guidelines:

1. Have a management or personal representative with you when you meet with the investigator.

2. Listen carefully to each question you are asked.

3. If you think the question is based on an incorrect assumption or otherwise inaccurate, say so. Explain your problem with the question, and make sure that your objections make it into any record the investigator is preparing if that question remains a part of the record.

4. You are obliged to cooperate with the investigator. But if you don't know an answer to one of the questions, say so. If you don't remember, say that. Tell the truth as accurately as you can recall it. But do not attempt to guess or fill in blanks if you do not truly know the answer to a question. *Remember, any statement you make now will remain part of the record as long as the complaint is being processed.*

5. It is your statement. If you don't feel the one the investigator has drafted is accurate or correct, prepare your own. *Never* sign anything you do not believe is accurate.

6. Take your time. Think over your answers. If you like, write down the questions and ask for time to compose your response—especially if you need to check records to give an accurate answer. A reasonable amount of time for you to reply includes time to consult with someone whose advice you trust.

7. Make sure all relevant facts become part of the investigator's record. If you decide to sign the statement prepared by an investigator, but do not think it sufficiently covers your position, supplement it with your documents and sworn statements.

Guidelines for Giving An EEO Statement

❏ **Have a representative with you**

❏ **Listen carefully to each question**

❏ **Question incorrect assumptions before answering the question**

❏ **If you don't know an answer—say so rather than guessing at the answer**

❏ **Do not sign a statement that is not accurate**

❏ **Take your time**

❏ **Ensure the relevant facts are part of the record**

❏ **Read the statement carefully**

❏ **Keep a copy of everything you sign or give to the investigator**

8. Before you sign anything, look it over carefully. Be sure it is accurate and that all dates and times are correct. It may also be a good idea to have it reviewed by someone else. You may be too close to the matter to be objective. Remember, if the wording does not properly reflect what you believe you said, you may re-word it the way you want. *It is your affidavit.*

9. Keep a copy of everything that you sign or provide to the investigator.

Results And Uses Of The Investigation

Complainants will receive a copy of the completed investigation report. The level and identity of the deciding official will vary between agencies. In some, the investigator makes a recommendation to the deciding official. In others the investigator provides a report without a recommendation. If one is made, the recommendation will state whether the complainant has established a *prima facie* case. All this means is whether the employee has brought forth evidence to leave a first impression that there may have been discrimination. It is **not** a final decision on the matter, particularly if the deciding official does not agree with the recommendation.

Although it is generally easy to build a *prima facie* case, some complaints are dismissed outright because, even if everything the employee filing the complaint says is accepted as being true and accurate, there would still be no legal basis for a finding of discrimination. For example, if an employee claimed that you did not promote him because he backed a rival football team, it may be true. But discrimination based on team preference is not prohibited by law. Not a good idea, but not actually illegal. In this example, even if the complainant's allegation was accepted as completely true, there would still not be a *prima facie* case, and the complaint would be dismissed.

If the deciding official determines that no discrimination occurred, the complainant will often be given an opportunity to drop the complaint. The complainant may be offered a settlement that grants some or all of the requested relief. If this happens, the matter will probably be informally resolved.

On the other hand, if there is a finding of no discrimination—which often happens—the agency must notify the complainant of the right to a hearing. The employee has 30 days from receipt of the report to request a hearing. The report of investigation will also be used in an attempt to informally resolve the complaint. It is very common at this point to enter into negotiations with the complainant to try and settle the problem. If this settlement effort is not successful, the agency will issue a "proposed disposition" of the complaint which will notify the complainant of her right to a hearing.

The Hearing

If the matter goes to an administrative hearing, an official of the Equal Employment Opportunity Commission (EEOC) will preside. The EEOC is a Federal agency with responsibility for equal employment opportunity matters both for the Federal Government and the private sector. This presiding official is known as an Administrative Judge. The judge is a full-time employee of the EEOC. The Administrative Judge will review the investigative file, consider any other evidence offered by the complainant or agency, and make a recommended decision to the agency head.

What To Expect At The Hearing

Although basically informal, such hearings operate like miniature trials. Witnesses—probably including yourself and the complainant, as well as others—will be called to testify. Witnesses are questioned first by a representative of their own side and then sometimes by the other side. Relevant documents are offered as evidence and discussed in testimony, and representatives usually make a final summary statement of how they think the case should be decided, and why.

"[N]ote that the *burden of proof* is on the complainant. Simply put, that means that you are presumed <u>not</u> to have discriminated until proven otherwise. There are no tie ball games."

Again, note that the *burden of proof* is on the complainant. Simply put, that means that you are presumed **not** to have discriminated until proven otherwise. There are no tie ball games. So, in general, you can expect the other side to go first to bring forward whatever evidence it feels indicates that discrimination took place. Then your agency's representative will be free to introduce evidence—testimony by witnesses, relevant documents, etc.—that will help to explain and show that your decisions and actions were taken for legitimate, non-discriminatory reasons.

Contrary to what you may expect from having watched courtroom dramas on television, such hearings are usually very low key affairs, without Perry Mason-like brow beating and tearful confessions. In any event, if you are to be involved in such a hearing, you can expect your agency's representative to work closely with you to prepare you to testify. You should remember that as a witness you should not expect to be present at the hearing during any time other than when you are personally testifying.

Being An Effective Witness

Remember the earlier discussion about keeping good records and documenting your reasons for taking—or not taking—action? This is where your records will pay off. Your agency is likely to assign an experienced advocate to defend the agency in the hearing and to get evidence into the record. Make sure the advocate understands the reasons for and the significance of your decisions.

Provide him with copies of all your records in the matter. And do not be afraid to point out what you believe are holes or weaknesses in the complainant's case that the advocate may have missed. *Remember, no one is likely to be as familiar with the facts in the case as you are! You are not required to be a silent participant in the process. If you have an opinion, speak up!*

You should also remember that the complaint is against the agency—not you. You may, however, be the agency's most valuable witness. The outcome of a case may be determined by an administrative judge's perception of the credibility of a witness.

There are a number of very important rules for witnesses to remember. Your advocate will probably review them with you before the hearing, but they are well worth repeating here:

➤ Tell the truth. Nothing is easier to unravel than a false statement. If the truth hurts (and it often does), its better to get it out and dealt with than to have it dragged out of you by the other side.

➤ Be yourself. Dress as you normally would for work. Speak as you normally do. In other words, be yourself!

➤ Listen carefully to questions and answer only the questions that you are asked to answer.

➤ Do not elaborate on answers requiring a simple yes or no.

➥ Do not volunteer information.

➥ Do not argue with the complainant's representative.

➥ If you don't know an answer, say so. If you don't remember a detail, say so. No one will expect you to have all of the answers, and guessing at answers when you are not sure will only hurt your credibility.

➥ If a question cannot be answered yes or no, say so and explain why.

➥ Stay calm and tell your story exactly as you remember it, in your own words.

Agency Head Decision

Based on the evidence in the record, the Administrative Judge from the Equal Employment Opportunity Commission will make a recommended finding to the head of your agency or whatever individual or group the agency head has designated to deal with such matters. The Agency Head or the person designated within your agency to handle such matters (this is often the EEO Officer in the agency) may accept or reject that finding. If a finding of discrimination is accepted, the agency will then focus on the appropriate remedy.

Appeal To The EEOC

A complainant may appeal the Agency head decision to the EEOC if the decision finds no discrimination, or if discrimination is found but the complainant is granted less relief than she seeks. Generally, however, the overwhelming majority of cases are resolved long before this point.

Appeal To The Courts

If the agency has not produced a file or made a final decision within 180 days of filing a formal complaint, the employee may initiate action in a Federal District Court.

An agency may not appeal an EEOC decision. However, a complainant may appeal to a U.S. District Court and higher if the case is significant and the complainant has the funds to pursue the matter. Again, only a very small percentage of cases proceed that far.

Settlement Essentials, Negotiation Strategies, And Options

Settlement of a discrimination complaint is an important option at every stage. If you are involved in in resolving discrimination complaints, the following points are important.

Settlement Essentials

1. An experienced advocate should be involved in any negotiations that may lead to a settlement.

2. The advocate should be one who has the confidence of management, and who has the authority to commit the agency within established limits.

3. The managers directly involved in any allegation usually should not participate directly in the settlement discussions. This is particularly true if the complainant will be a party to the meetings.

4. Careful planning of positions and offers you may be willing to make is crucial to the success of the discussions.

5. Establish your bottom line. Know the limits of management's willingness to settle the case.

Negotiation Strategies

1. Keep the discussions unemotional. Just as emotional managers usually make for unproductive negotiations, so can the presence of the complainant. Keep the discussions low key and businesslike.

2. It is the complainant who filed, so listen carefully while the representative explains how he perceives the case, its potential outcome and the desired relief.

3. Lower expectations without raising emotions. Use prior decisions to demonstrate what is reasonable to expect. Spell out the costs involved in future litigation and the uncertainty of the outcome.

4. If the complainant's representative is an attorney and the kind of case permits—age discrimination cases do not allow attorney fee awards for services provided in the administrative process—you may use an offer of attorney fees as an incentive to help settle the case. After all, if the complainant loses the case, the fees are the responsibility of the complainant.

5. Try to create a menu of options from which the complainant may select some, but not all choices. This encourages broader thinking and may get the person off the track of thinking in terms of a single unacceptable alternative.

6. Always conduct discussions in a conditional, trial balloon mode. This kind of discussion often gets the ball rolling and helps to keep your options open.

Options

In analyzing options for settlement, use your advocate or counsel to research the past cases involving similar allegations to ask:

> *What is the most an outside party (the EEOC or the courts) can give the complainant if we lose?*

The next logical question is:

> *What am I willing to give to resolve the matter quickly and avoid the time, expense and risk of going to an outside party for a decision?*

Other important factors are:

What will be the effects of a settlement, if any, on operations?

What about morale? What message will a settlement send to the work force?

What precedent would this settlement set, if any?

Will the settlement encourage more complaints?

On the positive side:

> A settlement gives a guaranteed result and ends the complaint. What is that worth?

> If the complaint has dragged on, will it clear the air in the organization?

> If it is early in the process, will a settlement avoid all the time and inconvenience of investigation and hearing?

Settlement is never easy, rarely pleasant and often costly. But it is a useful way for a manager to put potential problems to rest. And it can be an effective way of reducing both the costs and risks of further litigation.

If Discrimination Is Found...

A manager should always be prepared to counter a finding of discrimination with facts and evidence. Recognize that there may be cases where discrimination will be found—not necessarily because of any particular manager's action, but on the overall composition of the work force or on the fact finder's reading of the way your employees were treated.

A finding of discrimination does not usually carry a finding of intent to discriminate on the part of the manager. If you do get a decision that includes a finding of intent, however, the best advice available is to get a representative to protect your own interests.

Agencies generally take disciplinary actions only in those rare cases in which it is believed that an intent to discriminate can be proven. Such discipline may be appealed through agency procedures or, in more serious actions, to the Merit Systems Protection Board.

Under the Civil Rights Act of 1991, a Federal employee may seek compensatory damages of up to $300,000. Obviously, this means that you should seek advice from your agency advisors *before* embarking on any action that may lead to a meritorious complaint.

Do I Need A Representative?

The policy of most agencies in discrimination cases is to defend managerial decisions when those decisions were made pursuant to agency policies or regulations. Where the manager steps outside his or her authority, however, it should be understood that the manager is acting at his own peril.

The answer to the question "Do I need a representative?" is generally *yes*. If your agency does not provide representation, or if you believe that the agency representative will not adequately protect your own interests, seek an attorney or other person *experienced* in dealing with EEO matters to advise you.

Federal managers are entitled to representation when questioned by EEO investigators or at any hearing or other procedure where they will be required to make a statement under oath. Keep in mind that an agency representative that attends is there as the agency representative—not as your personal representative. Therefore, depending on the circumstances of your case, you may want to have your own attorney assist you.

Consequently, the answer to the question "do I need a representative?" is generally *yes*. If your agency does not provide representation, or if you believe that the agency representative will not adequately protect your own interests, seek an attorney or other person *experienced* in dealing with EEO matters to advise you.

Alternative Dispute Resolution

In October 1992, the Equal Employment Opportunity Commission changed its regulations controlling how discrimination complaints are to be processed in the Federal service. Although the changes were extensive and technical, there were really only two major areas that were modified that will have a direct, significant effect on you as a manager.

First, the Commission reduced the amount of time that an agency has to investigate and settle a complaint from one or two years to 180 days. (These new time limits are reflected in the discussion of handling complaints earlier in this book.)

Second, the new regulations encourage agencies to use *alternative dispute resolution* techniques (ADR) to resolve these controversies without having to engage in drawn out, expensive litigation (29 C.F.R. §1614.105(d)).

ADR is not new to the Federal Government. The Federal court system has been experimenting with different approaches to dispute resolution for a number of years. The benefits are obvious to almost everyone who has participated in ADR. When disputes are resolved early, the costs for litigation are reduced substantially, the harm to the parties is more limited and less expensive to remedy, and the matter is settled relatively quickly and does not hang around "forever" like in-laws after Christmas dinner.

In addition, ADR often results in the parties fashioning a remedy that satisfies them both, unlike the formal legal process that sometimes results in outcomes to no one's liking. Court decisions whether they be handed down by judges or juries are the result of an adversarial process with limited options. The purpose of the process is to make your claim look like it's the obviously correct answer, and to make any other claim look foolish, un-American, or just flat wrong. This public name calling often results in a decision and remedy that suggests that there was a winner and a loser (sometimes even two losers).

When cases go to resolution in the formal legal process, the court is restricted in what it can order as corrective action. Usually the legal remedies are an award of money, a direction that an employee be reinstated, or some other traditional "make whole" remedy. The attraction of ADR is that neither party is made out as the bad guy, and the only limit on a remedy is the imagination of the parties. If something other than money satisfies the person bringing the action, and the person being sued is willing to do whatever that is, then the matter is resolved with a lot less expense and a more effective resolution than it would have been if the matter had gone to court.

Why Is ADR Important To You?

Why is this important to you as a Federal manager? Very simply, because *you will be doing ADR* in an attempt to settle a discrimination complaint. The system pressures are just too great to resist. First, the EEOC has greatly reduced the time that an agency has to investigate and resolve discrimination complaints. Those agencies that in the past have taken several years to investigate a charge will now have to get everything done in six months. No agency will be able to do this just by working harder, it will have to work differently. ADR provides one of the few alternatives for agencies to resolve these cases within the new time limits.

Second, there's so much more money at stake now (up to $300,000 in most situations) that agencies will be looking for alternatives to litigation that do not necessarily involve large sums of money. ADR fills this requirement better than just about anything else available today. So any way that you look at it, ADR will become a part of your agency's discrimination process in the very near future, if it has not already.

ADR can take many forms; negotiation, fact-finding, arbitration, and mediation. The main trust of all these is that someone other than the supervisor and employee gets involved actively in helping the supervisor and the employee reach some settlement of the issue.

There are few rules involved in any of these forums, which means that there is a great deal of flexibility. And perhaps most importantly, the outcome is restricted to the case at hand and does not have an effect beyond the particular discrimination complaint in controversy.

Most Common ADR Form

The most common form of ADR today, and the forum most likely to be used initially by Federal agencies to settle discrimination complaints, is mediation. In mediation, someone not involved in the controversy meets with the supervisor(s) and employee who filed the complaint. The mediator's goal is to help both parties clarify the issues and to develop alternative solutions that will settle the discrimination complaint. It is not so important who is "right" or who is "wrong" in mediation. What is important is what can be done now to settle the matter without having to go to court.

Good mediators have three important characteristics: knowledge, trustworthiness, and creativity. The best mediators usually have extensive training and experience in helping people to resolve disagreements. In addition, they should be well versed in the "in's and out's" of Federal discrimination law. Because of this background, a good mediator will bring an important perspective and objectivity to a conflict that helps the parties to work together to resolve their differences.

The mediator has no authority to direct either the manager or the employee to do anything. He does not issue a decision on whether there actually was discrimination. His only tool is his ability to explain and convince.

If You Are Working With A Mediator...

If you become involved in working with a mediator, stay open to alternatives the mediator suggests. Early resolution of a discrimination complaint almost always works to the advantage of everyone, especially the involved manager. Even if you know that you did not discriminate, remind yourself that it may not be worth the effort that it will take to go all the way to the Supreme Court to prove that. Look for other ways to settle the issue. Use the mediator to your advantage as early as you can. More than one Federal manager has "gone to the mat" in defending some action against a charge of discrimination only to be told by a Federal judge that he was wrong.

Remember. Federal judges aren't always right. But they are always last. Do you *really* want to bet your career on what's going to happen in a court room? Mediation and the other forms of ADR can give you a convenient, effective, fair way to avoid this risk. Use them early and use them often.

KEY POINTS

➺ When a discrimination allegation is raised, keep your feelings in check. Remember, it is part of the job of being a Federal manager—try not to view it as a personal attack.

➺ Follow the rules for dealing with counselors and investigators. Prepare carefully, and cooperate in an effort to settle matters informally, if at all possible.

➺ If a complaint proceeds to more formal steps, obtain qualified representation and follow your representative's advice.

➺ Pursue settlements when doing so benefits all involved in the complaint.

➺ Remember, you are presumed innocent unless or until the evidence establishes otherwise.

Chapter Six

Additional
Information

Additional Useful Information

In dealing with EEO matters as part of your supervisory and managerial responsibilities, you will encounter a substantial number of terms that you may not be completely familiar with. Many of them have already been explained in earlier chapters. For example, you will encounter mention of terms like *prima facie* case, RMO, affirmative action plan, and Administrative Judge. To make it easy to refresh your memory as to what these terms mean, we have included both a brief glossary of terms and a brief outline of the various agency officials involved in administering your agency's EEO program.

GLOSSARY

Administrative File (EEO Complaint File)

Includes the complaint, counselor's report, letter accepting the complaint, report of the discrimination Complaints Investigator, and other documents relative to the complaint. If a hearing is to be conducted, this file is provided to the complainant and the Administrative Judge who will hear the case.

Administrative Judge

An employee of EEOC who conducts a hearing on the complaint and provides a recommended decision to the head of the agency.

Allegation

A claim that a decision or action involves or results in improper discrimination on a prohibited basis. Claims must be proven by supporting evidence.

Attorney Fees

If discrimination is found or the complaint is settled, the lawyer for the complainant generally requests payment for services. These fees are authorized in statute and regulation. Whether to pay and how much should be paid will depend on the circumstances of the case, the agency's objection to the fee, and in some cases, negotiations between the parties.

Burdens Of Proof And Production

Legal terms, these generally refer to what each party must establish to make their case. In other words, what the complainant or the agency must do at some point in a hearing or before a court to convince the judge they are right. The complainant always bears the burden of proof in EEO cases.

Class Action

A complaint alleging discrimination on a broad scale affecting a large number (more than thirty) of individuals. In a class action complaint all of the complainants allege the same basis for discrimination—such as age—and are entitled to the same relief if discrimination is found.

Corrective Action

Those actions taken by an agency as the result of a finding that discrimination occurred.

Make Whole Remedy

When discrimination is found this is generally the result. The agency must give the complainant whatever he or she would have been entitled to had the discrimination not taken place. This may include retroactive promotion, back pay, training or other actions on the part of the agency. It may also include attorney fees.

Handicap

Physical or mental impairment which substantially limits one or more of a person's major life activities. (From Rehabilitation Act). This may include addiction to alcohol or other controlled substance.

Hostile Environment

Generally used in connection with complaints of sexual harassment to describe the work situation created by sexually harassing superiors or coworkers.

Pretext

A claim by the complainant that the "legitimate reason" stated by the agency for taking an action was a subterfuge or cover for discrimination.

Neutral Policy

This applies to an agency rule that on its face appears not to discriminate but has a discriminatory effect on a particular group. For example, a language test that all employees must take might have a disproportionately adverse effect on Hispanic employees. Unless the requirement can be shown to be a valid job requirement, it will be held discriminatory.

Prima Facie Case

Literally means the "first face or impression." The first step in proving a case of discrimination. An example of a *prima facie* case would be one in which the complainant proved that he or she had applied for a job, had met the basic qualifications, but was not selected in favor of someone different in terms of race, color, sex etc. The agency may rebut such a case by proving that the selectee was better qualified or that it had some other legitimate reason for not selecting the complainant.

Reasonable Accommodation

Refers to the actions that must be taken by an agency to allow a disabled worker a reasonable opportunity to perform a particular job.

Record

Everything included in the evidence collected at a hearing, such as the investigative report, documents entered in evidence, and the testimony of witnesses.

Reverse Discrimination

Considered a misnomer by some, this refers to a case of discrimination filed by a white male. The law forbids discrimination and makes no distinction between races or sexes in who may become a victim of discrimination.

Agency EEO Programs and Officials

Director Of Equal Employment Opportunity

Each agency is required to have a Director of Equal Employment Opportunity. This individual is responsible both for submitting the agency's Affirmative Action plan to EEOC, and for assuring that the agency has appropriate regulations and policies on equal employment opportunity and complaint processing.

Equal Employment Opportunity (EEO) Officer

Some agencies call these positions deputy EEO Officers as authority may be delegated directly to a line manager. An EEO Officer's responsibility will vary according to the size of the organization. Generally, he or she will manage the organization's EEO program and the complaint process, supervise special emphasis program managers, and make or recommend decisions on the acceptance or rejection of discrimination complaints when first filed.

Federal Women's Program Manager (FWPM)

An advocate for women's issues in the organization, the FWPM will participate in development of the affirmative action plan, serve as a consultant to managers on Women's issues in the work place, and assist in recruitment and upward mobility efforts. The FWPM will often be active in developing training on EEO matters, including such issues as sexual harassment and the improvement of advancement opportunities for women.

Hispanic Employment Program Manager (HEPM)

The HEPM is responsible for increasing the number of Hispanic employees in the workforce and for improving the employment opportunities of current workers. This job also serves as a management consultant in dealing with such issues as cultural awareness and overcoming language barriers.

Handicap Program Officials

Agencies often devote one or more positions in the personnel office to the recruitment of disabled employees. If the organization is large or particularly involved in employing disabled workers, it is not unusual to have full time positions established to deal with issues involving disabled workers. These issues may range from planning necessary to remove architectural barriers, to efforts at restructuring positions to accommodate particular disabling conditions.

Equal Employment Opportunity Specialists

These positions may be involved in any aspect of the EEO program. Technically, each full time EEO Officer, Federal Women's Program Manager, Hispanic Employment Program Manager or Counselor is classified as an EEO Specialist.

Equal Employment Opportunity Counselor

A collateral duty position in all but the largest organizations, this position is responsible for dealing with allegations of discrimination before they become formal complaints. EEO Counselors attempt to identify issues brought to them by employees who believe they have been subject to discrimination. The counselor tries working with managers as a go-between to achieve an informal resolution to the allegation. A complaint cannot be made formal unless counseling has taken place. Counselors are required to submit a report of their efforts after the matter is resolved or a complaint is formalized.

Discrimination Complaint Investigator

When a formal complaint is accepted for investigation, the agency assigns a trained investigator who has the authority to gather documentary evidence relevant to the allegations, take sworn statements (affidavits) from those who have information on the matter, and in some agencies to make a preliminary finding of whether discrimination occurred. This finding is provided to a manager with authority to resolve the matter.

Source of EEO Rules

Who Makes The Rules

•• Congress, by the passage of laws, makes the rules. Several statutes deal specifically with discrimination in the Federal Government:

Where The Rules Are Located

•• Title VII of the Civil Rights Act of 1964(as amended)

•• The Age Discrimination in Employment Act of 1967(as amended)

•• The Equal Pay act of 1964 and Fair Labor Standards Act of 1938 (as amended)

•• The Rehabilitation Act of 1973 (Section 501)

•• The Equal Employment Opportunity Commission, by the issuance of regulations:

•• 29 CFR 1613 (EEO program and complaints), 1604 (sex), 1605 (religion), 1606 (national origin), and 1607 (employee selection procedures)

•• Agency regulations and management directives issued periodically

•• Court decisions, issued in connection with cases arising both in the public and private sector.

Affirmative Employment Plans

EEOC regulations require every agency to develop and submit affirmative employment plans. These plans must include:

Work Force Utilization Analysis

This is a profile of the work force by occupation, grade and category (race, age, sex etc.). Also included is a determination of underrepresentation (which groups in the work force do not reflect that group's participation in the population and general work force)

Statement Of Goals

This is established for each underrepresented group. It addresses the differences between the work force now in place and one in which there is full representation.

Analysis Of Barriers Or Impediments To EEO

Critical analysis of those factors within the agency's control which are impeding or may impede an effective EEO program.

Affirmative Employment Self-monitoring Plan

This plan involves showing how the agency will track its EEO efforts; what information systems need to be maintained; and what capabilities exist to evaluate program accomplishment.

Affirmative Employment Plan Summary

This is the actual plan in which the agency states what specific actions it will take each year as well as over the long run to accomplish equal employment opportunity goals.

KEY POINTS

Making EEO work for you involves:

•• Knowing the rules on discrimination and affirmative action

•• Making rational and defensible selections

•• Planning and implementing systems for your personnel decisions

•• Having objective performance and conduct expectations and communicating them to the workplace

•• Keeping prejudices and personal biases out of your decision making

•• Understanding the discrimination complaint process and how to react if your decision is the subject of a complaint

•• Being a mentor to your employees.

These are the crucial skills and abilities you need to make EEO work for you. Remember this is a manageable process and you are the manager to do it.

Newsletters From FPMI Communications, Inc.

The Federal Labor & Employee Relations Update

Subscription Fees:
>12 Months $195
>24 Months $360
>36 Months $495

>5 + Subscriptions $175 each
>10+ Subscriptions $155 each

The MSPB Alert

Subscription Fees:

>12 Months $125
>*LR Update subscribers pay only $95*

The Federal EEO Update

Subscription Fees:
>1-9 12 Month subscriptions $145 each
>10 + 12 Month subscriptions $125 each

The Federal Manager's Edge

Subscription Fees:
>1-50 12 Month subscriptions $65 each
>51-100 12 Month subscriptions $59 each
>101-500 12 Month subscriptions $52 each
>501-999 12 Month subscriptions $45 each
>1000+12 Month subscriptions $39 each

The Electronic Edge   (Minimum Order 50 subscriptions)

Subscription Fees:
>50-99 12 Month subscriptions $18.00 each
>100-199 12 Month subscriptions $11.00 each
>200-299 12 Month subscriptions $8.00 each
>300-399 12 Month subscriptions $7.00 each
>400-499 12 Month subscriptions $6.00 each
>500-999 12 Month subscriptions $5.00 each
>1000-2999 12 Month subscriptions $4.00 each
>3000-5000 12 Month subscriptions $3.00 each
>5000+ 12 Month subscriptions $2.00 each

Electronic Edge subscribers please indicate disk size

The Federal Power Curve

Subscription Fees:

> 1-99 12 Month subscriptions $295.00 each
> 100+ 12 Month subscriptions $150.00 each

The Federal Power Curve **(on disk)**

Subscription Fees:

> 50-100 12 Month subscriptions $150.00 each
> 101-200 12 Month subscriptions $100.00 each
> 201-300+12 Month subscriptions $ 81.67 each

> Electronic Power Curve subscribers please indicate disk size

To order or for information on quantity discounts, call FPMI
Communications on
(205) 539-1850 or fax (205) 539-9011.

Prices effective through December 31, 1994.

Video Training Packages
From FPMI Communications, Inc.

•Managing Cultural Diversity
> Package includes 25 guidebooks with workshops; a facilitators handbook with suggested workshop answers and a script with techniques to conduct a training session on cultural diversity; master copies of vu-graphs; and a 28 minute video on implementing cultural diversity in your agency. $695.00 for the complete set.

•Dealing With Misconduct
> Package includes video program, 25 guidebooks and 25 copies of *Federal Manager's Guide to Discipline* , ($695)

•Writing Effective Performance Standards
> Package includes video program, 25 guidebooks and 25 copies of *Performance Standards Made Simple* , ($695)

•Managing Under a Labor Agreement
•Managing Under The Labor Relations Law
> Special package includes both video programs with 25 workbooks for each course and 25 copies of *The Supervisors Guide to Federal Labor Relations* , ($895)

•Sexual Harassment: Not Government Approved
•Preventing Sexual Harassment: Some Practical Answers
> Order separate courses for $495.00 each. Or purchase our special package of both video programs with 25 workbooks and a leader's guide, 25 copies to *The Federal Supervisors Guide to Preventing Sexual Harassment* and *Sexual Harassment and the Federal Employee* , ($895)

Additional workbooks for each class are also available.

Quantity discounts are also available on all tape purchases. Call for more information.

Training Packages

•*Resolving Labor Management Relations Issues Through Partnership*
  Includes 25 copies of the Participant's Workbook,
  one copy of the Instructors Guide, 25 copies of the
  Supervisor's Guide to Federal Labor Relations and the
  Union Representatives Guide to Federal Labor Relations,
  plus master copies of overhead transparencies, ($595)

•*Practical Ethics Training for Government Managers and Employees*
  Includes 35 copies of the Participant's Workbook, 35
  copies of *Practical Ethics for The Federal Employee,*
  one copy of the Instructor's Guide, and master copies of
  more than 50 black & white overhead transparencies.
  ($595) Color transparencies and color slides available
  at additional cost.

•*Effective Equal Employment Opportunity Leadership*
  Includes 25 copies of the Participant's Workbook, 25 copies
  of the *Federal Employee's Guide to EEO,* 25 copies of the
  Federal Manager's Guide to EEO, one copy of the Instructor's
  Guide, master copies of more than 50 black & white overhead
  transparencies. ($595) Color transparencies and color slides
  available at additional cost.

Please call for more information on these packages. Quantity discounts
available. (205) 539-1850 or fax (205) 539-0911.

Publications from FPMI Communications, Inc.

• *The Bargaining Book* ($12.95)

• *Performance Standards Made Simple* ($8.95)

• *The Federal Employee's Guide to Drug Testing* (2nd Ed.) ($5.95)

• *The Federal Supervisor's Guide to Drug Testing* (2nd Ed.) ($8.95)

• *Federal Manager's Guide to Total Quality Management* ($8.95)

• *Managing the Civilian Workforce* ($8.95)

• *The Federal Manager's Survival Guide* (Military) ($8.95)

• *The Federal Manager's Survival Guide* (Regular) ($8.95)

• *The Federal Manager's Guide to Liability* ($8.95)

• *Effective Writing For Feds* ($8.95)

• *Practical Ethics for the Federal Employee* (2nd Ed.) $8.95)

• *Sexual Harassment and the Federal Employee* (2nd Ed.) ($5.95)

• *The Federal Manager's Guide to Preventing Sexual Harassment* (2nd Ed.) ($8.95)

• *The Federal Manager's Guide to EEO* (2nd Ed.) ($8.95)

• *Federal Employee's Guide to EEO* ($5.95)

• *Federal Manager's Guide to Leave and Attendance* (2nd Ed.) ($8.95)

• *Federal Manager's Guide to Discipline* (2nd Ed.) ($8.95)

• *The Ways of Wills* ($14.95)

• *The Federal Manager's Handbook* ($21.95)

• *Improving Employee Performance* ($8.95)

• *Supervisor's Guide to Federal Labor Relations* (3rd Ed.) $8.95)

• *Welcome to the Federal Government* ($6.95)

• *How ADR is used in the Federal Government* ($9.95)

• *A Practical Guide to Using ADR in the Federal Service* ($9.95)

• *RIF's and Furloughs: A Complete Guide to Rights and Procedures* (2nd Ed.) ($13.95)

•*Working Together: A Practical Guide to Labor-Management Partnerships* ($9.95)

•*A Practical Guide To IBB* ($9.95)

• *RIFs & Furloughs: A Complete Guide to Rights & Procedures* (2nd. Ed.) ($13.95)

Publications for Practitioners

•*Federal Employee's Law Practitioner's Handbook* (2nd Ed.) ($29.95)

•*The Desktop Guide to Unfair Labor Practices* ($25.00)

•*The Federal Practitioner's Guide to Negotiability* ($25.00)

•*The Union Representatives Guide to Federal Labor Relations* ($9.95)

•*Permissive Bargaining and Congressional Intent: A Special Report* ($19.95)

**SHIPPING: 1-10 Books: $3.50 11-50 Books $10.00
51+ Actual UPS Shipping Rates**

Training Seminars Available from FPMI

The Federal Personnel Management Institute, Inc. specializes in training seminars for Federal managers and supervisors. These seminars can be conducted at your worksite at a per person rate that is substantially less than open enrollment seminars.

The instructors for FPMI seminars have all had practical experience with the Federal Government and know problems Federal supervisors face and how to deal effective with those problems.

Some of the seminar-workshops available include:

- "Building Labor-Management Partnerships"

- "Interest Based Bargaining: New Approaches for Federal Negotiators"

- "Alternative Dispute Resolution: Resolving Workplace Conflict"

- "Labor Relations for Supervisors and Managers"

- "Developing Effective Performance Standards"

- "Managing Problem Employees"

- "Basic Labor Relations Workshop"

- "Negotiating An Effective Labor Agreement"

- "Legal Writing for Personnelists and EEO Specialists"

- "Handling ULP Disputes"

- "Conducting Fact-Finding and Administrative Investigations"

FPMI, Inc.
707 Fiber Street
Huntsville, AL 35801

Phone (205) 539-1850 • Fax (205) 539-0911

The Federal Labor & Employee
Relations Update

This is the monthly newsletter used by the government for keeping up-to-date on case decisions and events affecting labor relations in the federal government.

Each Issue contains new case decisions from the FLRA, MSPB, and the Federal Service Impasses Panel that affect you and your agency—plus articles on issues affecting the federal labor and employee relations community.

Update subscriptions are only $195.00 per year (12 issues) and quantity discounts are available to enable your agency to provide copies for all personnel professionals in your agency.

To start your subscription or to receive a complimentary review copy of the *Update*, just fax the enclosed form to FPMI Communications on (205) 539-0911 or send it to:

FPMI Communications, Inc.
707 Fiber Street
Huntsville, AL 35801-5833

☐Please start my subscription right away.
☐Please send one complimentary issue for my review.

Name:
Title:
Agency & Organization:
City, State, Zip:
Phone:

Prices and Offer Good Through December 31, 1994